PUBLIC RIGHTS OF WAY:
The Essential Law

PUBLIC RIGHTS OF WAY:
The Essential Law

Angela Sydenham

WS
&H

Wildy, Simmonds & Hill Publishing

ISBN: 9780854902088

British Library Cataloguing in Publication Data

A catalogue record for this book is available from the British Library

First published in 2019 by

Wildy, Simmonds & Hill Publishing
Wildy & Sons Ltd
Lincoln's Inn Archway
Carey Street
London WC2A 2JD
www.wildy.com

Typeset by Heather Jones, North Petherton, Somerset.
Printed in Great Britain by Ashford Colour Press, Unit 600, Fareham Reach, Fareham Road, Gosport, Hampshire PO13 0FW.

Contents

Preface

This book is an introduction to the complex area of public rights of way. It is aimed at practitioners, lawyers and surveyors, who are not necessarily experts in this area of the law, but who may have to deal with rights of way in conveyancing transactions, land management or planning matters. It is hoped that the book will also be useful for landowners, farmers, members of the public and those working for local authorities.

For this reason, the book does not follow the conventional pattern of dividing the chapters into subject topics, but looks at the law from the angle of the landowner, the purchaser, the public users of the rights and the local authority. There will, of course, be some chapters which will be relevant to all parties.

Sections 20 to 26 of, and Schedule 7 to, the Deregulation Act 2015 will introduce many changes to the recording of public rights of way. The provisions were originally expected to come into force in April 2016. Although the relevant regulations are still awaited, the book covers the prospective legislation.

I am grateful to my former Birkett colleagues, Nigel Farthing (property litigation partner specialising in public rights of way, commons and village greens) and Carol Ramsden (joining as a Rights of Way Executive, now a Senior Associate specialising in public rights of way; Fellow of the Institute of Public Rights of Way and Countryside Access Management) for their expertise and their continuing stimulating conversations in my retirement.

Last, but not least, a big thank you to Andrew Riddoch at Wildy, Simmonds & Hill Publishing and Heather Jones, who has been the most meticulous and helpful copy-editor I have ever worked with. I first suggested this book to Andrew in 2015, but due to the lack of implementation of the Deregulation Act provisions, I lost heart and did not proceed. Then, in 2018, fearing I would not live to see the relevant legislation in force, I approached Wildy again. Much to my surprise, not only Andrew did not complain of my delay in submitting my text, but he also agreed to publish the book at this late stage.

The law stated is as of 1 March 2019.

Angela Sydenham
Aldeburgh

Table of Cases

References are to page numbers.

Table of Statutes

References are to page numbers.

Table of Statutory Instruments

References are to page numbers.

Table of EU Material

References are to page numbers.

Table of Other Material

References are to page numbers.

List of Abbreviations

AONB	Area of outstanding natural beauty
BOAT	Byway open to all traffic
CA 1968	Countryside Act 1968
Convention on Human Rights	European Convention for the Protection of Human Rights and Fundamental Freedoms 1950
CROWA 2000	Countryside and Rights of Way Act 2000
DA 2015	Deregulation Act 2015
Defra	Department for Environment, Food and Rural Affairs
DETR	Department for the Environment, Transport and the Regions
HA 1980	Highways Act 1980
HSE	Health and Safety Executive
MCAA 2009	Marine and Coastal Access Act 2009
NERCA 2006	Natural Environment and Rural Communities Act 2006
NPACA 1949	National Parks and Access to the Countryside Act 1949
RUPP	Road used as public path
SI 1995/451 Regulations	Rail Crossing Extinguishment and Diversion Orders, the Public Path Orders and the Definitive Maps and Statements (Amendment) Regulations 1995
SSSI	Site of Special Scientific Interest
TCPA 1990	Town and Country Planning Act 1990
WLCA 1981	Wildlife and Countryside Act 1981

1 Basic Information

1.1 Introduction

A public right of way is a highway. The terms 'highway' and 'public right of way' are used interchangeably, although sometimes the term 'highway' is used to denote the physical route rather than the right itself. The legal consequence of land being a highway is that the public have a right to pass and repass along a linear route.

There is a legal maxim, 'Once a highway always a highway'. This means that unless a path has been extinguished or diverted by a statutory enactment, it will continue to exist. This is so even if the path has not been used for many years and even if there is no physical evidence on the ground of its existence.

1.2 Sources

1.2.1 Introduction

The law relating to public rights of way is founded on common law and statute. Much of the detail is set out in regulations. The statutes which deal with highways and public rights of way are numerous. Set out below are the main statutes which are relevant today.

1.2.2 Highways Act 1980

The Highways Act 1980 (HA 1980) deals with the law relating to highways generally including public rights of way. There are important sections dealing with changes to the network: creation, diversion and extinguishment orders. Many of the provisions relating to highway offences also apply to public rights of way.

1.2.3 Wildlife and Countryside Act 1981

Part III of, and Schedules 14, 15 and 16 to, the Wildlife and Countryside Act 1981 (WLCA 1981) deal with the recording of rights of way on the definitive map held by the surveying authority. The WLCA 1981 also covers provisions on signposting, wardens and the keeping of bulls on land crossed by rights of way.

1.2.4 Countryside and Rights of Way Act 2000

Part II of, and Schedules 5 and 6 to, the Countryside and Rights of Way Act 2000 (CROWA 2000) contain provisions relating to public rights of way which amend both the HA 1980 and the WLCA 1981. Included are the re-designation of roads used as public paths (RUPPs) as restricted byways, the extinguishment (cut-off) of certain unrecorded rights of way and the requirement for local highway authorities to prepare and publish improvement plans for the rights of way in their area. There are also provisions dealing with the obstruction of public rights of way.

1.2.5 Natural Environment and Rural Communities Act 2006

Subject to exceptions, the Natural Environment and Rural Communities Act 2006 (NERCA 2006) limits the creation of new public rights of way for mechanically propelled vehicles and extinguishes such existing rights as are unrecorded. The NERCA 2006 amends the HA 1980 to ensure that use for a period of at least 20 years of a way by a non-mechanically propelled vehicle (such as a pedal cycle) can create in appropriate circumstances a public right of way for non-mechanically propelled vehicles (a restricted byway).

1.2.6 Marine and Coastal Access Act 2009

Part 9 of the Marine and Coastal Access Act 2009 (MCAA 2009) imposes a duty on the Secretary of State and Natural England to provide a route around the whole of the English coast consisting of one or more long-distance routes on foot or by ferry and a margin of land in association with the route available to the public for recreational journeys.

1.2.7 Growth and Infrastructure Act 2013

The Growth and Infrastructure Act 2013 makes amendments to applications under the Town and Country Planning Act 1990 (TCPA 1990) for stopping up and diversion orders to enable development.

The Act also makes amendments to section 31 of the HA 1980 which enables landowners to lodge statements showing their lack of intention to dedicate rights of way.

1.2.8 Deregulation Act 2015

In the words of the Explanatory Notes to the Deregulation Act 2015 (DA 2015), '[t]he Deregulation Act 2015 provides for the removal or reduction of burdens on businesses, civil society, individuals, public sector bodies and the taxpayer'. The DA 2015 makes several amendments to existing legislation on public rights of way.

Sections 20 to 26 of (and Schedule 7 to) the DA 2015 contain amendments to the HA 1980, the WLCA 1981 and the CROWA 2000. These include alterations on procedures for public path and definitive map orders and greater protection from extinguishment of rights of way. The power to authorise gates at the landowner's request is extended to byways.

These provisions will apply in England only, not in Wales.

However, although it was anticipated that the provisions together with regulations would come into effect in 2016, this has not happened. There must be some doubt as to whether the sections will ever be brought into force.

1.3 Advice

The Department for Environment, Food and Rural Affairs (Defra) has produced guidance on many aspects of the law and practice. Information relating to public rights of way is to be found on the government website.

1.4 Glossary

Bridleway	A right of way on foot, riding or leading a horse, and may include a right to drive animals. The Countryside Act 1968 provides that bicyclists may use a bridleway.
Byway open to all traffic	A right of way 'for vehicular and all other kinds of traffic but which is used by the public mainly for the purpose for which footpaths and bridleways are so used'.
Carriageway	A right of way for vehicles and lesser forms of traffic.
Church ways	Ways not available to the general public, but for parishioners to gain access to church.
Coastal access	Long-distance route and margin provided under the MCAA 2009.
CROWA 2000 access	Access to registered common land, mapped open country and coastal margin.
Cycle tracks	Cycle Tracks Act 1984 enables footpaths to be converted into cycle tracks.

Definitive map	Map of public rights of way maintained by the surveying authority.
Ferries	These may link highways separated by water.
Footpath	A right of way on foot.
Fords	Land is defined in the HA 1980 to include land covered by water.
Foreshore	There is no common law right to walk on the foreshore, but a right of way may have been dedicated or there may be permissive use.
Green Lanes	This is a non-legal term referring to the physical description of an unsurfaced track.
Highway	A right over a defined linear route for the public to pass and repass.
Long-distance path	Created under the National Parks and Access to the Countryside Act 1949.
Motor vehicle	Mechanically propelled vehicle intended or adapted for use on roads.
Occupation roads	Roads laid out for the use of the occupiers of particular lands.
Permissive paths	A licensed right of way provided on a permissive basis by the landowner.
Private right of way	This is an easement: a right of way for the benefit of a particular piece of land. It cannot be used by the general public.
Public right of way	A right over a defined linear route for the public to pass and repass.
Railways	The rail track is not a public right of way.
Restricted byway	A right of way for non-mechanically propelled vehicles.
River	Considered a highway for some purposes, but is not covered by the deemed dedication provisions now in section 31 of the HA 1980.
Road	Defined differently in different statutes. The term does not necessarily imply a public right of way for vehicles.
Street	Defined differently in different statutes.
Town and village green	Access provided for local inhabitants to indulge in lawful sports and pastimes.
Towpaths	These are not public rights of way unless dedicated expressly or by long use.

2 Rights of the Public

2.1 Meaning of 'public'

For a highway to exist, there must be a right of passage for the public at large, not a section of the public.[1]

A highway may be contrasted with a private right of way, or easement, for the benefit of some nearby land. Sometimes there are accommodation roads for several adjoining landowners. There are also church ways or local roads, available for parishioners of a particular parish or manor, which do not amount to highways.

2.2 Defined route

The right of passage must exist over a defined route. A route may be sufficiently defined if it varies from time to time.[2] There cannot be a public right to wander (*ius spatiendi*) at common law.[3] Although such a right may be created by statute or agreement, it will not create highway rights.

The defined route does not have to lead anywhere. It can be a cul-de-sac.[4] However, when considering evidence as to whether a highway exists, it will be relevant to consider the purpose of such a highway. If it does not connect to another highway, or a place of popular resort, such as a river,[5] the sea[6] or a beauty spot,[7] this may strengthen an argument against the existence of a highway,[8] or that the highway continued further. The existence, or creation, of a cul-de-sac route will also be a relevant

---

1 *Poole v Huskinson* (1843) 11 M&W 827.

2 *Fernlee Estates v City and Council of Swansea and National Assembly for Wales* [2001] P&CR 19; see also *Wimbledon & Putney Commons Conservators v Dixon* (1875) 1 Ch D 362 (way across open land divided into parallel routes).

3 *A-G v Antrobus* [1905] 2 Ch 188.

4 *Rugby Charity Trustees v Merryweather* (1790) 11 East 375n.

5 *R v St Issey Inhabitants* (1849) 14 LT(OS) 176.

6 *Williams-Ellis v Cobb* [1935] 1 KB 310.

7 *Eyre v New Forest Highway Board* (1892) 56 JP 517; *Moser v Ambleside UDC* (1925) 89 JP 118.

8 *Roberts v Webster* (1967) 66 LGR 298.

consideration when a local authority is deciding whether to make a public path order.[9]

In order to establish a public right of way, either at common law or under section 31 of the HA 1980, at least one terminus must join a public right of way.[10]

2.3 Nature of the right

The public have no legal interest in the land itself. But they do have a right to pass and repass along the route. Any other activity, unless it is incidental to the right of passage, will be a trespass or may amount to an obstruction.

Permitted incidental activities include parking a car on a vehicular highway, resting, stopping for refreshments, taking photographs and making a sketch. On the other hand, interfering with a game drive[11] or observing the performance of race horses on adjoining land[12] has been held to be a trespass. Metal detecting would also be a trespass.[13]

A procession will not normally amount to an obstruction unless it unreasonably restricts the rights of other highway users or amounts to a nuisance. A static meeting is more likely to amount to an obstruction. Where a proposed public procession is to demonstrate support for, or opposition to, the views or actions of any body or persons, to publicise a cause or campaign or mark or commemorate a campaign an event, prior written notice must be given to the police.[14]

The rights of the public have been enhanced and complicated by reliance on the European Convention for the Protection of Human Rights and Fundamental Freedoms 1950 (Convention on Human Rights). There have been several cases concerning assemblies on highways. In *DPP v Jones and Another*,[15] the House of Lords held that an assembly on a highway, even though it was not ancillary to the exercise of a right of passage, was a

---

9 See HA 1980, s 119(2), and Defra, Rights of Way Circular 1/09, 'Guidance for Local Authorities' (Defra, 2009) paras 5.48 and 7.18.

10 *Kotegaonkar v Secretary of State for the Environment Food and Rural Affairs* [2012] EWHC 1976 (Admin).

11 *Harrison v Rutland* [1893] 1 QB 142.

12 *Hickman v Maisey* [1900] 1 QB 752.

13 *Waverley Borough Council v Fletcher* [1995] 4 All ER 756. Metal detecting on a scheduled site is an offence: Ancient Monuments and Archaeological Areas Act 1979, s 42.

14 Public Order Act 1986, s 11. *Kay v Commissioner of Police of the Metropolis* [2008] UKHL 69 (no need to give notice as came within the exception of s 119).

15 [1999] 2 WLR 625.

reasonable use of the highway provided it did not interfere with other users and was not a public or private nuisance. In *Westminster City Council v Haw*,[16] the fact that Haw had numerous placards and posters as well as a bed on the pavement was held not to be an unreasonable use of the highway. No pedestrian had been obstructed in his right of passage. It was accepted that Haw was exercising his freedom of expression under Article 10 of the Convention on Human Rights. Other factors which influenced the decision were the purpose, place and duration of the obstruction.

A much publicised case was *Mayor, Commonality and Citizens of the City of London v Samede, Barda, Ashman and persons unknown*,[17] which concerned a protest camp which was set up on highway land outside St Paul's Cathedral. The court granted orders for possession of the land and injunctive and declaratory relief for the removal of the tents, dismissing arguments based on Articles 10 and 11 of the Convention on Human Rights. Whether an assembly on a highway is lawful depends on the factual situation. In refusing leave to appeal against the High Court decision, the Master of the Rolls expressed the position as follows:[18]

> In our view, [the] factors include (but are not limited to) the extent to which the continuation of the protest would breach domestic law, the importance of the precise location to the protestors, the duration of the protest, the degree to which the protestors occupy the land, and the extent of the actual interference the protest causes to the rights of others, including the property rights of the owners of the land, and the rights of any members of the public.

2.4 Categories of public rights of way

2.4.1 A carriageway, including a byway open to all traffic

A carriageway and byway open to all traffic (BOAT) give the public a right of passage with vehicles. As there is a general principle of law that the greater includes the lesser right, the public may also use a carriageway on horse and on foot.[19] This rule is subject to specific statutory exceptions; for example, the rules governing use of motorways.

---

16 [2002] EWHC 2073 (QB).

17 [2012] EWHC 34 (QB).

18 [2012] EWCA Civ 160, [39].

19 *R v Hatfield (Inhabitants)* (1736) Lee Temp Hard 315; *Wells v London, Tilbury and Southend Rail Co* (1877) 5 Ch D 126.

Although there is a presumption that there is a right to drive animals along carriageways, the presumption may be rebutted.[20]

BOATs are a special sub-category of carriageways which are recorded on definitive maps. The definition is as follows:[21]

> ... 'byway open to all traffic' means a highway over which the public have a right of way for vehicular and all other kinds of traffic, but which is used by the public mainly for the purposes for which footpaths and bridleways are so used.

Part 6 of the NERCA 2006 prevents any use after 2 May 2006 of a way by mechanically propelled vehicles from giving rise to any future public rights of way. New public rights of way for mechanically propelled vehicles will be created only if they are granted expressly, or if they relate to a road constructed expressly for that purpose.[22] Existing public rights of way for mechanically propelled vehicles, where those rights are not recorded on the definitive map and statement, will, subject to exceptions, be extinguished.

2.4.2 A restricted byway

On a restricted byway, the public have a right of way on foot, on horseback and leading a horse, and a right for vehicles other than mechanically propelled vehicles.[23] A mechanically propelled vehicle does not include an electrically assisted pedal cycle. The rights are referred to in the CROWA 2000 as restricted byway rights. The public may also have a right to drive animals of any description along a restricted byway. Such rights would have to be proved.

A highway can be a restricted byway even if it is at the side of a river, canal or other inland navigation, and the public have the right to use it in connection with navigation.

2.4.3 A bridleway

A bridleway is defined as:[24]

> ... a highway over which the public have the following, but no other, rights of way, that is to say, a right of way on foot and a right of way on horseback

---

20 *Ballard v Dyson* (1808) 1 Taunt 279.

21 WLCA 1981, s 66(1). The term was first introduced in the Countryside Act 1968 (CA 1968).

22 NERC 2006, s 66.

23 CROWA 2000, s 48; WLCA 1981, s 53(4A) and (4B).

24 WLCA 1981, s 66(1); HA 1980, s 329(1).

> or leading a horse, with or without a right to drive animals of any description along the highway.

'Horse' is defined to include pony, ass or mule,[25] but not llama.

Whether driftway rights (i.e. a right to drive animals) exist will depend on the evidence.

The rights have been extended by the Countryside Act 1968 (CA 1968) to include the right to ride a bicycle, but not 'a mechanically propelled vehicle intended or adapted for use on roads'.[26] In exercising their rights, cyclists must give way to pedestrians and horse riders.[27] Cycle riding may be forbidden by local orders or byelaws.[28]

2.4.4 A footpath

The public have a right of way on foot only over a footpath.[29]

Questions which often arise over footpaths are what the walker can take with him. It was said in *R v Mathias*[30] that a person may take:

> ... such things as are usual accompaniments of a large class of foot passengers, being so small and light, as neither to be a nuisance to other passengers nor injurious to the soil.

In that case, the jury decided that a perambulator was a usual accompaniment.

Dogs are regarded as a usual accompaniment, although this has not been tested by the courts. There are, however, several offences relating to dogs. Of particular relevance is the Dog (Protection of Livestock) Act 1953. It is an offence under this Act to allow a dog to be at large in a field or enclosure where there are sheep. If a dog is on enclosed land where there are sheep it must be kept on a lead or under close control. A dog attacking sheep would be out of control and could be shot by a farmer.

---

25 WLCA 1981, s 66(1); HA 1980, s 329(1).

26 Road Traffic Act 1988, Sch 3, para 5.

27 CA 1968, s 30. The reference to bicycle, rather than cycle, seems to restrict it to two-wheeled cycles.

28 Local Government Act 1972, s 235.

29 WLCA 1981, s 66(1).

30 (1861) 2 F&F 570, 175 ER 1191.

2.5 Nature of trespass

Trespass is a civil wrong. Except where statute has made it so – for instance, trespass onto railway land – it is not a crime.[31] The remedy for trespass is damages. Where no physical damage has occurred, the damages are likely to be nominal only. Persistent trespassers may be restrained by an injunction.

If a trespasser declines to leave land on request, the occupier may physically eject him provided no more force is used than is reasonably necessary. This course of action is not, however, recommended. Use of excessive force can result in criminal or civil proceedings being brought against the ejector or his agents.

A properly maintained path, well waymarked, should cut down the incidents of trespass. It is not always easy to follow maps when the position is not clear on the ground. Many users will not have maps with them. Entry by a walker onto adjoining land will generally amount to trespass. However, if a right of way is obstructed by the owner of the land, the path user may deviate onto other land in the same ownership adjoining the path in order to get around the obstruction.[32] There is no right for the public to deviate where the obstruction arises from natural causes or the path has been destroyed by erosion.[33] It would also be a trespass to use a public right of way for metal detecting.

Where the surface is vested in the highway authority, the trespass will be against the authority. In *Wiltshire County Council v Frazer*,[34] the county council was held able to bring summary proceedings against squatters who had put their caravans on the highway.

There may also be a trespass where greater rights than those established on a public right of way are exercised. Thus, it would be a trespass to ride a horse or bicycle on a footpath or to drive on a public right of way without vehicular rights if the activity were carried on without the consent of the landowner.

---

31 Railway Regulations Act 1840, s 16.

32 *Stacey v Sherrin* (1913) 29 TLR 555; *Dawes v Hawkins* (1860) 8CB (NS) 848.

33 *R (Gloucestershire CC) v Secretary of State for the Environment, Transport and the Regions* (2001) 82 P&CR 15. *Dicta* to the contrary in *Taylor v Whitehead* (1781) 2 Doug KB 745 can no longer be considered valid.

34 (1984) 47 P&CR 69.

2.6 Which routes can the public use?

The public can use routes which have been dedicated as rights of way, either expressly or by implied dedication, or which have been created by a public path order. The creation of public rights of way is covered in Chapter 3.

The definitive map, held by local authorities, shows those public rights of way which have been recorded. Ordnance Survey maps also show public rights of way. The highway authority is under a duty to erect and maintain a signpost where a footpath, bridleway or byway leaves a metalled road.[35]

There may be perfectly valid rights of way which have not been recorded. Members of the public who have documentary evidence of the existence of a path, or are able to prove user as of right (i.e. without force, secrecy or permission), may apply to the surveying authority for a modification order to rectify the definitive map.

The duties of the authority on receiving such an application are set out in Chapter 8.

---

35 CA 1968, s 27(2).

3 Creation of Rights of Way

3.1 Introduction

Highways may be created by statute or by dedication and acceptance, either at common law or by statutory presumption. Statutes provide for highways to be created on construction, by declaration, by agreement and by order. The principal statute under which highways are constructed today is the HA 1980. The normal procedure is for the highway authority to acquire the land by agreement or under compulsory powers.[1] Once constructed, the way automatically becomes a highway without any dedication or acceptance.[2]

Private carriageways, whether in existence or to be constructed, may also be adopted so that they become highways. An agreement is made by the persons who have the capacity to dedicate the highway and the highway authority.[3] Where the road is to be constructed, the agreement will provide that it should be constructed to a specified standard. Once adopted, the road becomes publicly maintainable.

Section 34 of the HA 1980 enables a county council, a metropolitan district council, a London borough council or the Common Council of the City of London to make a declaration that a street which is not a highway and land treated as a street shall become a highway. Footpaths, bridleways and restricted byways are usually created by agreements or orders or by dedication and acceptance.[4]

---

1 HA 1980, Pt XII; Acquisition of Land Act 1981.

2 *R v Lyon* (1825) 5 Dow & Ry KB 497.

3 HA 1980, s 38.

4 HA 1980, ss 25 and 26; Restricted Byways (Application and Consequential Amendment of Provisions) Regulations 2006 (SI 2006/1177).

3.2 Public path creation agreements

3.2.1 Local authority agreements

Footpaths, bridleways and restricted byways may be created by the landowner and local authority.[5] 'Local authority' is defined to include county councils and district councils, and in Greater London, a London Borough or the Common Council. Section 25 has been extended to the Norfolk and Suffolk Broads Authority and National Park authorities.[6]

The agreement may provide for payments to be made to the landowner and for the dedication of the public path to be subject to limitations or conditions affecting the public right of way over it.[7]

Before entering into the agreement, the local authority must consult any other local authorities in whose area the land is situated. It does not have to consult parish councils or the public. It is also the duty of the local authority to have due regard to the needs of agriculture and forestry and the desirability of conserving flora, fauna and geographical and physiographical features. 'Agriculture' includes the breeding and keeping of horses.[8]

Once the agreement has been made, the local authority is obliged to take all necessary steps to ensure that the restricted byway, bridleway or footpath is dedicated in accordance with the agreement.

Where a path is created by a public path creation agreement, or an order is made by a local authority which is not the highway authority for the path, or by the Secretary of State, the highway authority must survey the path and certify what work is necessary to make it in a fit condition for use by the public. The certificate must be served on the local authority or Secretary of State. The highway authority must carry out the works, but can recover the expenses of so doing from the authority on whom the notice was served. Alternatively, with the consent of the highway authority, the local authority can perform the duties imposed on the

---

5 HA 1980, s 25(1); Restricted Byways (Application and Consequential Amendment of Provisions) Regulations 2006 (SI 2006/1177).

6 HA 1980, s 25(2); Norfolk and Suffolk Broads Act 1988, s 2(5) and (6), s 23(2) and Sch 3, para 47(1); Environment Act 1995, ss 70 and 125(2) and Sch 9, para 11(a); Restricted Byways (Application and Consequential Amendment of Provisions) Regulations 2006 (SI 2006/1177).

7 HA 1980, s 25. An example of a limitation would where the path passes through a gate or stile (which otherwise would be an obstruction).

8 HA 1980, s 29, as amended by CROWA 2000, Sch 6, Pt I, para 2.

highway authority and carry out the works.[9] Section 38(6) of the HA 1980 has been held to include future maintenance.[10]

The path automatically becomes maintainable at public expense.

3.2.2 Parish and community council agreements

Parish and community councils have power to enter into agreements for the creation of highways with those who have the capacity to dedicate public rights of way, over land in the parish or community or an adjoining parish or community.[11]

The dedication must, in the opinion of the council, be beneficial to the inhabitants of the parish or community. The council is under no obligation to take into account the needs of agriculture, forestry or conservation issues when agreeing a path.

There is no power for the parish or community to make a payment for the paths to be dedicated. However, there is power for the councils to carry out works including works of maintenance or improvement, or to contribute to the expense of carrying out such works, but the path is not automatically maintainable at public expense.

There is no obligation to see that the path is set out physically or to publish its existence.

3.3 Public path creation orders

3.3.1 Orders for public right of way purposes

Unitary authorities, district and county councils, National Park authorities, London borough councils and the Common Council of the City of London have power to make orders for the creation of footpaths, bridleways and restricted byways.[12]

---

9 HA 1980, s 27.

10 *R (Redrow Homes Ltd) v Knowsley Metropolitan Borough Council* [2014] EWCA Civ 1433.

11 HA 1980, s 30.

12 HA 1980, s 26; Restricted Byways (Application and Consequential Amendment of Provisions) Regulations 2006 (SI 2006/1177). See Rights of Way Review Committee Practice Guidance Notes, PGN1, 'Consultation on changes to public rights of way and definitive maps' (5th edn, November 2008). In exercising their functions, public authorities are subject to the Disability Discrimination Act 2005.

It must appear to the council that there is a need for the new path, and it must be satisfied that it is expedient to create a new path having regard to:

(1) the extent to which it would add to the convenience or enjoyment of a substantial section of the public or of local residents; and

(2) the effect which the creation order would have on the rights of those with an interest in the land, taking into account the provisions for compensation.[13]

The council must consult with other local authorities in whose area the land is situated.

The Secretary of State may also make creation orders, provided they comply with the tests set out above. He must consult with the relevant local authorities. The Secretary of State, when deciding whether to make or confirm an order, and the local authority, when deciding whether to confirm an unopposed order, must have regard to the rights of way improvement plan for the area.[14]

The public path order may create a public path unconditionally or subject to conditions or limitations. The procedure which must be followed is set out in the HA 1980.[15] The order must be in the form prescribed by regulations.[16] As with creation agreements, the local authority must have due regard to the needs of agriculture and forestry and the desirability of conserving flora, fauna and geological and physiographical features in making the order.[17]

The order made by the authority must subsequently be confirmed by the authority or, where objections are made, by the Secretary of State.[18] There are no separate tests for the confirmation as distinct from the making of a creation order as there are for the making and confirmation of a diversion or extinguishment order. However, the Secretary of State, in deciding whether to make or confirm an order, and the local authority, in deciding

---

13 HA 1980, ss 26 and 28. Section 26 'requires [the] tests to be applied both in respect of the footpath but also to the details of its alignment, length and width'. *R (MJI (Farming) Ltd) v Secretary of State for Food, Environment and Rural Affairs* [2009] EWHC 677 (Admin), [25].

14 HA 1980, s 26(3A), inserted by CROWA 2000, Sch 6.

15 HA 1980, s 26(3A), inserted by CROWA 2000, Sch 6.

16 Public Path Orders Regulations 1993 (SI 1993/11). See also Defra, Rights of Way Circular 1/09, 'Guidance for Local Authorities' (Defra, 2009).

17 HA 1980, s 29, as amended by CROWA 2000, Sch 6, Pt I, para 2.

18 An authority may decide in the face of opposition to withdraw the order and not refer it to the Secretary of State. See *R (Hargrave) v Stroud District Council* [2002] EWCA Civ 1281.

whether to confirm an unopposed order, must take into account any improvement plan for the area.[19]

Before an order is confirmed, the local authority, or the Secretary of State where he has made the order, must give notice in the prescribed form, stating the general effect of the order, naming the place where a copy of the order and the map may be inspected and specifying the time within which any objections may be made. In England, the notice must be publicised on a website maintained by the authority or through the use of such other digital communications media as the authority may consider appropriate. In Wales, the notice must be published in at least one local newspaper circulating in the area.[20] Notice must also be served on affected owners, occupiers, councils and other specified persons. Copies of the notice must be displayed on the proposed path and in the local council offices.

New paths may be created as part of the reorganisation of the network. Concurrent orders may be made which create, divert and extinguish paths. The highway authority must do what is necessary to make up the new path or arrange that the order-making authority does so.[21]

Compensation is payable to the landowner if the value of his land has been depreciated or if he has suffered damage by being disturbed in his enjoyment of land by the coming into effect of the creation order. Disputes on the amount of compensation are decided by the Upper Tribunal (Lands Chamber).[22]

3.3.2 Applications for purposes of access to open land and registered common land

Natural England may make an application to the Secretary of State for a public path creation order to enable the public to obtain access, or to facilitate such access, to land within the meaning of Part 1 of the CROWA 2000. In Wales, the application is made by Natural Resources Wales to the Welsh Ministers.[23]

---

19 HA 1980, s 26 as amended by CROWA 2000, Sch 6, Pt I, para 1. See also s 85(1) (special considerations to be taken into account in areas of outstanding natural beauty (AONBs)).

20 HA 1980, Sch 6, para 1(3ZA). Inserted by DA 2015, Sch 7, Pt 4, para 8 (not yet in force).

21 HA 1980, s 27.

22 HA 1980, ss 28 and 307(1).

23 CROWA 2000, s 58(1).

Before Natural England or Natural Resources Wales makes the request, it must have regard to any rights of way improvement plan prepared by the local highway authority for the relevant area.[24]

3.4 Dedication and acceptance

3.4.1 Expressed or implied

A landowner may expressly dedicate a right of way. The dedication must be in perpetuity.[25] It cannot be for a term of years. The dedication may be made subject to limitations. For example, a right of way may be dedicated subject to gates or the right to hold fairs or markets.[26] There must also be acceptance by the public.[27] The historical reason for this is that, before 1835, all highways were repairable by the inhabitants of the parish. It was therefore considered that a landowner, by dedicating a route, should not impose liability on the local inhabitants unless the route was shown to be of use to them.

A highway authority has power to accept a highway on behalf of the public. Acceptance by the highway authority is capable therefore of amounting to proof of acceptance by the public. Examples are where a highway authority agrees in writing to accept a dedication or where an appropriate committee of the highway authority agrees to do so.[28]

Although new highways are today normally created under statutory provisions, recourse to the common law rules is necessary to establish whether disputed rights of way were dedicated in the past.

Use by the public may not only be evidence of acceptance of a dedicated route, but also evidence of dedication itself. Long use may give rise to an inferred dedication at common law (where the onus is on the claimant to establish that the landowner dedicated the route as a public right of way) or a statutory deemed dedication under the HA 1980[29] (where after 20 years' use before the right of way is brought into question the onus is on the landowner to show he had no intention to dedicate).

---

[24] CROWA 2000, s 58(2).

[25] *Dawes v Hawkins* (1860) 8 CB NS 848.

[26] *Attorney General v Horner* (1885) 11 App Cas 66.

[27] *R v Mellor* (1830) 1 Lew CC 158; *Cubitt v Maxse* (1873) LR 8 CP 704.

[28] *Secretary of State for the Environment, Transport and the Regions v Baylis (Gloucester) Ltd* [2000] 2 EGLR 13.

[29] HA 1980, s 31.

3.4.2 User as of right

In order for there to be an inferred dedication at common law or deemed dedication under the HA 1980, the user must be as of right. This means that the user must be without force (*nec vi*), secrecy (*nec clam*) or permission (*nec precario*).[30] This is similar to the requirement for obtaining a private right of way by prescription and for making an application for a Class C village green which is created by use. The courts have resisted arguments for additional tests over and beyond the tripartite test.[31] Many recent cases on user as of right have been concerned with applications for village greens.

The user will not be without force if it is necessary to break locks or fences or if the user is contentious or subject to protest.[32] In *R (Lewis) v Redcar and Cleveland Borough Council*, Lord Rodger stated,[33] 'If the use continues despite the neighbour's protests and attempts to interrupt it, it is treated as being *vi*... user is only peaceable (*nec vi*) if it is neither violent or contentious'. Notices, forbidding access or stating 'No right of way', may, depending on the facts, make the user contentious. The notices should be clear and explicit.[34] It is necessary to have in place a system for regular inspection and replacement for damaged or missing signs.

User will be secret if the route is used only at night or when it is known that the landowner or his agent is away.

The user will be permissive as far as employees and invitees are concerned or where tolls are paid.[35] Byelaws, in a village green case, were held to amount to an implied permission.[36]

---

30 *Earl De la Warr v Miles* (1881) 17 Ch D 535, 596; *Gardner v Hodgsons's Kingston Brewery Ltd* [1903] AC 229, 239.

31 *R (Lewis) v Redcar and Cleveland Borough Council* [2010] UKSC 11; *Powell and Irani v Secretary of State for the Environment, Food and Rural Affairs* [2014] EWHC 4009 (Admin).

32 *Eaton v Swansea Waterworks Co* (1851) 17 QB 267; *Dalton v Angus & Co* (1881) 6 App Cas 740, 786.

33 [2010] UKSC 11, [89] and [90].

34 For a discussion of the effectiveness of notices in relation to village greens, see *Betterment Properties (Weymouth Limited) v Dorset County Council* [2010] EWHC 3045 (Ch). See also *R (Oxfordshire & Buckinghamshire Mental Health NHS Foundation Trust) v Oxfordshire County Council* [2010] EWHC 530 (Admin).

35 *R v Secretary of State for the Environment ex parte Cowell* [1993] JPL 851.

36 *R (Newhaven Port and Properties Ltd) v East Sussex County Council & Newhaven Town Council* [2015] UKSC 7.

User by virtue of some statutory provision is treated as permissive. It is not user as of right, but user by right.[37] Similarly, where a public right of way is recorded on the definitive map, whether or not in error, there can be no claim to user as of right. The use of the path by the public is by virtue of the entry on the map, i.e. by right, not as of right. The landowner is not in a position to stop the use.[38]

On the other hand, where a footpath had been diverted by an order, but no modification had been made to the definitive map and statement, a claim for a public right of way over the former route was upheld on the basis of twenty years' use.[39]

The requirement of user as of right was summed up by Lord Blackburn in *Mann v Brodie*.[40] He said:

> Where there has been evidence of a user by the public so long and in such a manner that the owner of the field, whoever he was, must have been aware that the public were acting under the belief that the way had been dedicated, and has taken no steps to disabuse them of their belief, it is not conclusive evidence, but evidence on which those who have to find a fact may find that there was a dedication by the owner whoever he was.

However, the subjective belief of the users themselves has subsequently been held to be immaterial. This point has been firmly established by the House of Lords in the case of *R v Oxfordshire County Council ex parte Sunningwell Parish Council*.[41]

Lord Hoffmann said:

> A person who believes he has the right to use a footpath will use it in the way in which a person having such a right would use it. But user which is apparently as of right cannot be discounted merely because, as will often be the case, many of the users over a long period were subjectively indifferent as to whether a right existed, or even had private knowledge that it did not.

---

37 *Barkas v North Yorkshire County Council and Scarborough Council* [2014] UKSC 31.

38 See Defra, Rights of Way Circular 1/09, 'Guidance for Local Authorities' (Defra, 2009) para 4.30 *et seq.*

39 *Powell v Irani v Secretary of State for the Environment, Food and Rural affairs* [2014] EWHC 4009 (Admin).

40 (1885) 10 App Cases 378, 386.

41 [1999] 3 WLR 160, 171.

3.4.3 The public at large

The dedication of a way must be to the public at large, not to a particular class of persons. Some paths, such as church paths, may be available for a particular purpose, and their use may be limited, say, to the parishioners. However, the acceptance does not have to be by all members of the public. It is sufficient for a highway to be created if it is used by a section of the public.

In *R v Broke*[42] the court decided that use by seafarers of a path amounted to use by the public. There is a distinction between a grant to the public, when the path must be made available for all Her Majesty's subjects, and user by the public. User can therefore be established for the purposes of common law dedication even if the route has been used only by local inhabitants, as long as there is nothing to prevent it being used by anyone. This point was made by Coleridge CJ in *R v Inhabitants of Southampton*,[43] where he explained that user by the public 'must not be taken in its widest sense; it cannot mean that it is a user by all the subjects of the Queen, for it is common knowledge that in many cases it is only the residents in the neighbourhood who ever use a particular road or bridge'.

Often, a public right of way may have been established for a purpose which no longer exists. For instance, it may have provided a route for people to get to a village shop which has subsequently been converted into a house or to a place of work which has been closed. Provided there was a genuine public right of way, rather than merely a permissive route, the right of way continues to have legal existence. It matters not that the route is used for recreational purposes only.

The laying out of estate roads for the use of those living on the estate will not amount to dedication. Although the road may be used by postmen, meter readers, tradesmen and so on, they will be using the road not as members of the general public, but as invitees or licensees.[44]

It is possible that a road which was originally used as an estate road may subsequently be used by the public. However, the courts will look more closely at the degree of user where the route started off as a private road.[45]

---

42 (1859) 1 F&F 514. See also *R v Inhabitants of Southampton* (1887) 19 QBD 590.

43 (1887) 19 QBD 590.

44 *Selby v Crystal Palace Gas Co* (1862) 4 DeGF&J 246.

45 See Neville J in *Holloway v Egham UDC* (1908) 72 JP 433, 434.

3.4.4 Use by mechanically propelled vehicles[46]

There are several statutes that make it an offence to drive on land. Two of these are of particular importance for rights of way: section 193 of the Law of Property Act 1925 and section 34 of the Road Traffic Act 1988.

Section 193 of the Law of Property Act 1925 makes it an offence for any person to draw or drive without lawful authority on land, to which the section applies, any carriage, cart, caravan, truck or other vehicle. The section applies to metropolitan commons within the meaning of the Metropolitan Commons Acts 1866–1898 or commons which, immediately before 1 April 1974, were wholly or partly in a borough or urban district. It also applies to land where the owner of the soil has declared by deed that the section will apply.

Section 34 of the Road Traffic Act 1988[47] provides:

(1) Subject to the provisions of this section, if without lawful authority a person drives a mechanically propelled vehicle:

  (a) on or upon any common land, moorland, or land of any other description, not being land forming part of a road, or

  (b) on any road being a footpath, a bridleway or restricted byway,

 he is guilty of an offence.

(2) It is not an offence under this section to drive a mechanically propelled vehicle on any land within fifteen yards of a road, being a road on which a motor vehicle may lawfully be driven, for the purpose only of parking the vehicle on that land.

'Road' is defined in the Road Traffic Act 1988 as 'any highway and any other road to which the public has access'.[48] Section 34 is a very wide section and covers most types of land.[49]

Under both statutes, the offence is committed only where the driving takes place without lawful authority. In *Hanning v Top Deck Travel*,[50] the court held that no prescriptive right could arise because it would be contrary to

---

46 'Mechanically propelled vehicle does not include a vehicle falling within section 189(1)(c) of the Road Traffic Act 1988 (electrically-assisted pedal cycle)', HA 1980, s 31(12), as inserted by NERCA 2006, s 68(4).

47 As amended by CROWA 2000, s 67 and Sch 7.

48 Road Traffic Act 1988, s 192.

49 See *Massey v Boulden* [2002] EWCA Civ 1634, where the *eiusdem generis* rule was held not to apply to the wording in Road Traffic Act 1988, s 34(1)(b).

50 (1993) 68 P&CR 14.

statute. However, the decision in *Hanning v Top Deck Travel* was overruled by *Bakewell Management Ltd v Brandwood*.[51] A landowner has lawful authority to grant a private right of way, and so a right can arise from long use, as it is based on a presumed grant. By analogy, a public right of way could also arise by long use. User as of right, in the absence of a lack of intention to dedicate, could be evidence of dedication.

On the other hand, if a landowner cannot expressly grant a private right of way or dedicate a public right of way, then one cannot arise from long use. It is not open to a landowner to dedicate a vehicular route if to do so would cause a public nuisance to those using a public footpath. Stuart-Smith LJ in *Hereford and Worcester County Council v Pick*[52] said that the user relied on was not only contrary to statute (and therefore, as the law was understood at the time, could not be relied on), but also would have constituted a public nuisance to pedestrians using the footpath, and so for that reason also could not lead to a presumed dedication.

The same argument would apply to the dedication of a new vehicular right over a green. The use would be likely to interfere with the persons using the green. Moreover, section 12 of the Inclosure Act 1857 makes it an offence to cause injury to, or to commit a nuisance on, a town or village green. Under section 29 of the Commons Act 1876, any encroachment on, or inclosure of, a town or village green and any disturbance to the green otherwise than with a view to its better enjoyment is deemed to be a public nuisance. There is no defence of lawful authority as there is under section 193 of the Law of Property Act 1925 or section 34 of the Road Traffic Act 1988. Therefore, it is unlikely that a public right of way can arise by an implied common law dedication or a deemed statutory dedication.

Part 6 of NERCA 2006 has introduced provisions to make it more difficult to obtain a right of way on any land for mechanically propelled vehicles by implied or deemed dedication.[53] It has prevented any use by a mechanically propelled vehicle after 2 May 2006[54] from giving rise in the future to any kind of public right of way (i.e. it will not give rise to a footpath, bridleway, restricted byway or BOAT). New public rights of way for mechanically propelled vehicles will be created only if they are granted

---

51 [2004] UKHL 14, [2004] 2 AC 519.

52 (1995) 71 P&CR 231.

53 NERCA 2006, ss 66–71.

54 The commencement date of the section in England. In Wales, the commencement date was 16 November 2006.

expressly, or if they relate to a road intended to be used by mechanically propelled vehicles and constructed for that purpose under an enactment.[55]

Where there is evidence of a qualifying period of use by non-mechanical vehicles, such as a horse and cart or bicycle, a restricted byway may be created.[56]

3.4.5 User which may upgrade footpaths and bridleways

Use by horse riders of a footpath is a trespass against the landowner, but not a criminal offence.[57] Bridleway rights may be acquired over a footpath by long use. Nor is it a criminal offence to drive a horse and cart on a footpath or bridleway. Long use is capable of converting a footpath or bridleway into a restricted byway. However, such a deemed dedication does not impose any additional maintenance burdens on the highway authority or any other persons.[58]

3.4.6 Bicycles

Bicycles are allowed on bridleways by virtue of the CA 1968.[59] However, in exercising that right, cyclists must give way to pedestrians and persons on horseback. The right may be prohibited or restricted by byelaws or local authority orders. Highway authorities are not under any obligation to make or maintain bridleways so that they are suitable for bicycles.

There is no right to ride a bicycle on a footpath. Anyone doing so would be committing a trespass against the landowner. However, it is not a criminal offence. As bicycles are not a natural accompaniment of a walker, pushing a bicycle would be a trespass. Carrying a bicycle should not be a trespass as there is no physical contact with the ground and the burden on the path is not increased.

Were a sufficient number of people to ride a bicycle over a defined route or on a public footpath, this could amount to a deemed dedication of a

---

55 NERCA 2006, s 66.

56 NERCA 2006, s 68.

57 The user could of course commit criminal offences on the land by his other activities on the land, e.g. under the Criminal Damage Act 1971.

58 NERCA 2006, s 68(3), inserting s 31(10A) into the HA 1980.

59 CA 1968, s 30.

restricted byway.[60] A mechanically propelled vehicle does not include an electrically assisted pedal cycle.[61]

In *Whitworth v Secretary of State for the Environment, Food and Rural Affairs*,[62] an application for a restricted byway based on use of a bridleway by pedal cycles was rejected on the grounds that the user was by right under section 30 of the CA 1968. Lord Carnwath suggested obiter that even if there had not been evidence of an existing bridleway, use by bicycles might result in a bridleway rather than a restricted byway. He said:

> It is true that regular use by both horse-riders and cyclists over that period would be consistent with an assumed dedication as a restricted byway at the beginning of the period (had that concept then existed). But it is no less consistent with an assumed dedication as a bridleway, of which cyclists have been able to take advantage under the 1968 Act. Since section 30 involves a statutory interference with private property rights, it is appropriate in my view, other things being equal, to infer the form of dedication by the owner which is least burdensome to him.

This seems a doubtful proposition.

Section 3 of the Cycle Tracks Act 1984 enables a footpath to be converted into a cycle track by a conversion order. The procedure for making a conversion order is set out in regulations.[63] The Act provides that any person having a legal interest in agricultural land, which the footpath crosses, must have consented in writing to the order.[64] There is a duty before making the order to consult with the organisations which represent persons using the footpath, other parochial authorities, any statutory undertakers whose property is crossed by the footpath and the chief police officer for the area. Compensation is payable if the land is depreciated by the creation of the track or damage is caused by the conversion work.[65]

3.5 Inferred dedication at common law

3.5.1 Intention

A landowner must have an intention to dedicate a right of way over his land. Public user may be evidence from which that intention may be inferred. This reflects the policy of the courts to uphold long use and

---

60 NERCA 2006, s 68.

61 NERCA 2006, s 68(4), inserting s 31(12) into the HA 1980.

62 [2010] EWCA Civ 1468.

63 Cycle Tracks Regulations 1984 (SI 1984/1431).

64 Cycle Tracks Act 1984, s 4.

65 Cycle Tracks Act 1984, s 5.

assume it has a lawful origin. This is shown in other areas of law, such as the prescriptive right to easements and the upholding of customary rights on village greens. However, mere use does not create the highway; dedication is required.[66]

The courts have, in some instances, refused to imply dedication where they can find that the use has been as a result of the tolerance of land owners, 'It is the wise policy of the law, not to construe acts of charity, though continued and repeated for never so many years, in such a manner as to make them the foundation of legal obligations', per Heath J in *Steel v Houghton*.[67]

It is possible that what was originally tolerance, over the years, may turn into intention to dedicate.

Where the public has deviated onto adjoining land because of the poor condition of the right of way, this will not usually create a new route.[68]

3.5.2 Burden of proof

Where there is a claim that a public right of way has been dedicated, it is for the claimant to prove that it can be inferred by the landowner's conduct that he had actually dedicated the route as a public right of way.[69] User of right is not of itself necessarily sufficient. As stated above, it is still possible that the use was due to the landowner's tolerance rather than his intention to dedicate the route, or that there is evidence of the landlord's lack of intention to dedicate.[70]

3.5.3 Length and quality of user

The length of enjoyment which must be shown depends on the circumstances. In one case, 18 months was held to be sufficient.[71]

---

66 *Attorney-General v Esher Linoleum Company Ltd* [1901] 2 Ch 647.

67 (1788) 1 Hy Bl 51, 60. See, however, *R v Oxfordshire County Council ex parte Sunningwell Parish Council* [1999] 3 WLR 160, and *R (Beresford) v Sunderland County Council* [2003] UKHL 60 for the distinction between tolerance and permission. For a recent case where tolerance was relevant, see *Slough Borough Council v Secretary of State for Environment, Food and Rural Affairs* [2018] EWHC 1963 (Admin).

68 *Dawes v Hawkins* (1860) 8 CB NS 848.

69 *Jaques v Secretary of State for the Environment* [1995] JPEL 1031. See also *R v Lloyd* (1808) 1 Camp 260, 170 ER 1191, and *Folkestone Corpn v Brockman* [1914] AC 338.

70 *Folkestone Corpn v Brockman* [1914] AC 338.

71 *North London Rail Co v St Mary, Islington Vestry* (1827) 27 LT 672.

The amount of user (i.e. the number of people who have used a route) also has not been defined and will be considered in the light of the particular facts. The essential element is that it should be obvious to the landowner that a route was being used by the public.

3.5.4 Rebutting dedication

A landowner, or a tenant,[72] may prevent a right of way being established across his land. He can put up physical barriers, erect notices indicating that the route is private,[73] turn people back and lodge statements and declarations with the highway authority.[74] Objections at a public inquiry by persons who may or may not have been the landowners at the time were held to be sufficient evidence to rebut dedication where there was future use of the route.[75]

In *Poole v Huskinson*, Park B said, 'A single act of interruption by a landowner is of much more weight, upon the question of intention, than many acts of enjoyment'.[76] Notices rebutting dedication have to be absolutely clear.[77] A notice with the words 'Private Road – Access only' was held insufficient to rebut an intention to dedicate the route as a footpath or bridleway.[78] A notice on adjoining land stating 'Trespassers will be prosecuted', besides being incorrect, would also be ineffective.

Where notices valid under section 31(3) are torn down or defaced, a notice given by the landowner to the appropriate council that the way is not

---

72 *Rowley v Secretary of State for Transport, Local Government and the Regions* [2002] EWHC 1040 (Admin).

73 HA 1980, s 31(3). On ambiguous notices, see *Burrows v Secretary of State for Environment Food and Rural Affairs* [2004] EWHC 132 (Admin).

74 HA 1980, s 31(6).

75 *Wild v Secretary of State for Environment, Food and Rural Affairs* [2009] EWCA Civ 1406. Cf *Paterson v Secretary of State for Food, Environment and Rural Affairs and Oxfordshire County Council and the Ramblers Association* [2010] EWHC 394 (Admin) (a case on statutory deemed dedication where an intention not to dedicate shown before the start of a 20-year period did not operate to oust the statutory presumption that arose from the use during that period).

76 (1843) 11 M&W 827, 830.

77 For a discussion on the effectiveness of notices in relation to village greens, see *Betterment Properties (Weymouth Limited) v Dorset County Council* [2010] EWHC 3045 (Ch).

78 *Burrows v Secretary of State for the Environment, Food and Rural Affairs* [2004] EWHC 132 (Admin).

dedicated as a highway, in the absence of evidence of a contrary intention, is sufficient evidence of his intention not to dedicate.[79]

Gates put across a route may indicate that the landowner has no intention to dedicate a right of way. However, other interpretations are possible. The purpose of the gates may be to control stock, not deter the public; or the right of way may have been dedicated subject to the gate or other obstruction.[80]

Shutting the path for at least one day a year has been accepted as a standard method of showing an intention not to dedicate.[81] The fact that the path is to be closed should be brought to the attention of the public. However, where a door was locked on a path leading to shops and businesses closed over the Christmas period, this was held not to be sufficient evidence of lack of intention to dedicate.[82]

In order to rebut dedication, there must be overt and contemporaneous acts[83] by the landowner to show that he has no intention to dedicate. It is not sufficient for him merely to state that he had no such intention.

In the words of Lord Denning:[84]

> In my opinion a landowner cannot escape the effect of 20 years' prescription by saying that, locked in his own mind, he had no intention to dedicate it: or by telling a stranger to the locality (who had no reason to dispute it) that he had no intention to dedicate. In order for there to be 'sufficient evidence that there was no intention' to dedicate the way, there must be evidence of some overt acts on the part of the landowner such as show the public at large – the public who use the path, in this case the villagers – that he had no intention to dedicate. He must, in Lord Blackburn's words, take steps to disabuse those persons of any belief that there was a public right: see *Mann v Brodie*, 10 App Cas 378, 386 ...

---

79 HA 1980, s 31(5). In *Paterson v Secretary of State for Food, Environment and Rural Affairs and Oxfordshire County Council and the Ramblers Association* [2010] EWHC 394 (Admin), the terms of a letter sent to the rural district council were held not to comply with the section.

80 *Barraclough v Johnson* (1838) 8 A&E 99.

81 *Rugby Charity Trustees v Merryweather* (1790) 11 East 375n; *British Museum Trustees v Finnis* (1833) 4 C&P 460.

82 *Ali v Secretary of State for Environment, Food and Rural Affairs* [2015] EWHC 893 (Admin).

83 Cf *Norman and Bird v Secretary of State for Environment and Rural Affairs* [2006] EWHC 1881 (Admin), where Collins J stated that the question was whether the landlord's lack of intention was supported by sufficient evidence. An overt and contemporaneous act was not something which was, as a matter of law, needed in order to establish sufficient evidence.

84 *Fairey v Southampton County Council* [1956] 2 QB 439, 458.

Although Lord Denning refers to the 20-year period under what is now the HA 1980, his words would equally have applied to dedication at common law.

Lord Denning's words have been quoted with approval by Lord Hoffmann in *R (Godmanchester Town Council) v Secretary of State for the Environment Food and Rural Affairs and Cambridge County Council* and *R (Drain) v Secretary of State for Environment Food and Rural Affairs and Yattendon Estates Ltd*,[85] who continued by stating:

> I think that upon the true construction of section 31(1) 'intention' means that the relevant audience, namely the users of the way, would reasonably have understood the landowner's intention to be. The test is … objective: not what the owner subjectively intended nor what particular users of the way subjectively assumed, but whether a reasonable user would have understood that the owner was intending, as Lord Blackburn put it in *Mann v Brodie* 10 App Cas 378, 386, to 'disabuse [him]' of the notion that the way was a public highway.

The effect of the House of Lords' decision is that *R v Secretary of State ex parte Billson*[86] is no longer good law. Both a challenge, which brings a right of way into question for the purposes of section 31(1) of the HA 1980, and the lack of intention to dedicate must be brought home to the public. However, *Godmanchester* and *Drain* also established that it is sufficient if the landowner's lack of intention to dedicate was shown for part of the 20-year period. It did not have to be shown throughout the 20 years.

If the land is let on either a fixed-term tenancy or a periodic yearly tenancy, the person entitled to the reversion (i.e. the freeholder or a person with a superior leasehold interest) has the right, notwithstanding the existence of the tenancy, to put up a notice. However, in doing so, he must not injure the business or occupation of the tenant.[87] The lessee, being in exclusive possession of the land, needs no statutory authority to erect any notices.

The most important method of rebutting deemed dedication is the lodging with the appropriate council of a map and statement indicating what ways, if any, the landowner admits to having dedicated as highways. In the absence of a contrary intention, a declaration to the effect that no additional ways, other than those mentioned in the declaration, over the land have been dedicated as highways, since the lodging of the statement and map (and previous declaration, if any) is sufficient evidence to

---

85 [2007] UKHL 28.

86 [1999] QB 374. User held permissive where, unknown to the public, a landowner had executed a deed under Law of Property Act 1925, s 193 giving a right of access.

87 HA 1980, s 31(4).

negative the intention of the owner or his successors in title to dedicate any additional ways as highways.[88]

The HA 1980 in England, but not in Wales, has been amended by the Growth and Infrastructure Act 2013. The rules therefore differ.

In England, the map and statement and subsequent declaration must be in the prescribed form. The declaration must be lodged within 20 years of the deposit or subsequent declaration.[89]

In Wales, the map should be of a scale of not less than 6 inches to the mile (1:10,560).[90] The subsequent declaration must be a statutory declaration.[91] It must be lodged with the appropriate council within 10 years.

The statement and declaration should be made by the owner. 'Owner' is defined as the person who is for the time being entitled to dispose of the fee simple of the land.[92]

It is important to stress that this procedure rebuts any intention of dedication in the future only. It cannot take away any claims which are based on past user. Nor will it overcome any claims based on documentary evidence. The effect of lodging a statement may lead to an application being made to add additional ways to the definitive map on the basis of user before the date of the statement or on the strength of documentary evidence. In other words, it may galvanise a member of the public into action.

The appropriate council is required to keep a register of deposited maps, statements and declarations lodged with that council. Regulations[93] provide for the format and contents of the register and the circumstances when entries relating to a map, statement or declaration may be removed. The register must be available for inspection free of charge at all reasonable hours.[94]

The Secretary of State has been given power to make regulations for land in England for a statement and declaration to be combined with a statement under section 15A of the Commons Act 2006 and for the fees

---

88 HA 1980, s 31(6).

89 HA 1980, s 31(6a).

90 HA 1980, s 31(6b).

91 HA 1980, s 31(6b).

92 HA 1980, s 31(7).

93 Dedicated Highways (Register under Section 31A of the Highways Act) (England) Regulations 2007 (SI 2007/2334) amended by Commons (Registration of Town or Village Greens) and Dedicated Highways (Landowner Statements and Declarations) (England) Regulations 2013 (SI 2013/1774).

94 HA 1980, s 31A, inserted by CROWA 2000, Sch 6, Pt I, para 4.

payable for lodging statements and declarations.[95] Section 15A enables a landowner to lodge a statement which has the effect of bringing to an end any period during which persons may have indulged, as of right, in lawful sports and pastimes on the land. Regulations have been made governing the making of the application, the timing of the deposit, management and publication of the application, under section 15B(1) of the Commons Act 2006, the manner of keeping the register and the removal of entries from the register.[96]

3.5.5 Capacity

Although a person may have an expressed or implied intention to dedicate, such a dedication will be ineffective if that person does not have the legal capacity to do so. Generally speaking, it will be the fee simple owner (i.e. the person with the legal estate) who will be able to dedicate a right of way.

3.6 Statutory deemed dedication

3.6.1 Introduction

Statutory deemed dedication was first introduced by the Rights of Way Act 1932. This Act has now been replaced by section 31 of the HA 1980.

There may be circumstances where it is not possible to rely on this section of the HA 1980. The Act does not apply to the Crown, the Duchies of Lancaster and Cornwall, the Forestry Commission and government departments, which count as the Crown; or there may be less than 20 years' use, or the use which is relied on may not immediately pre-date the event which brings the right of way into question. In such circumstances, reliance will have to be placed on common law dedication. Section 31(9) provides:

> Nothing in this section operates to prevent the dedication of a way as a highway being presumed on use for less than 20 years, or being presumed or proved in any circumstances in which it might have been presumed or proved immediately before the commencement of this Act.

---

95 HA 1980, s 31(13), inserted by Growth and Infrastructure Act 2013, s 13.

96 Commons (Registration of Town or Village Greens) and Dedicated Highways (Landowner Statements and Declarations) (England) Regulations 2013 (SI 2013/1774). Defra has issued guidance 'Guidance to Commons Registration Authorities in England on Sections 15A to 15C of the Commons Act 2006' (Defra, revised in December 2016), and 'Guidance on the completion of Form CA16' (Defra, 2013).

Section 31 is retrospective and applies to user both before and after the Act came into force. In *Fairey v Southampton County Council*,[97] a right of way was brought into question in 1931. Twenty years' user was shown before that date, and it was held that the path could validly be shown on the definitive map.

3.6.2 Section 31(1) of the Highways Act 1980

The section provides:

> Where *a way over land*, other than *a way of such a character* that use of it by the public could not give rise at common law to any presumption of dedication, has been actually enjoyed by the public *as of right* and *without interruption* for a full period of 20 years, the way is deemed to have been dedicated as a highway unless there is sufficient evidence that there was no intention during that period to dedicate it. [emphasis added]

As with inferred dedication at common law, there must be user as of right by the public at large and not sufficient evidence of lack of intention to dedicate, but the main difference is the burden of proof. At common law, the claimant has to show that the landowner intended, or could be presumed to have intended, to dedicate a public right of way. Under the statute, it is for the landowner to rebut the presumption.

The words emphasised above need special explanation.

A way over land

It has been held that section 31 does not apply to rivers. However, rivers are treated as highways for some purposes, and long use can give rise to navigation rights at common law.

A way of such a character

Section 31 stipulates that the statutory presumption will not apply where there is 'a way of such a character that use of it by the public could not give rise at common law to any presumption of dedication'.

The meaning of this phrase is obscure. It may cover situations such as paths through churchyards. As it has been held that the use of the word 'way' in the section refers to the physical way[98] and not the legal right of way, it does not appear to cover any lack of capacity of landowners with limited interest. It is possible that it would cover situations where a landowner could not expressly grant a right of way as it would be contrary

---

97 [1956] 2 QB 439.

98 *Attorney General (ex rel Yorkshire Derwent Trust) v Brotherton* [1992] 1 AC 425.

to statute[99] or such a grant would constitute a public nuisance. What is clear is that section 31 does not apply to right of navigation over rivers. Although the Act defines 'land' to include land covered with water, this has been interpreted to mean fords, not rivers where the right is over water rather than land.[100]

In *Kotegaonkar v Secretary of State for the Environment, Food and Rural Affairs*,[101] a route between two privately owned sites, a health centre at one end and a row of shops at the other, was held not to be a public highway, either at common law or under section 31 of the HA 1980, because members of the public had no legal right of entry at either end of the path; they entered the health centre and the shops under licence from the respective landowners, not because they had an unrestricted right to do so. Neither end of the claimed path joined a public right of way.

As of right

This is discussed at 3.4.2 in relation to common law dedication. The requirement that the user is without force, secrecy or permission gives rise to much litigation not only in the context of public rights of way, but also in relation to private rights of way and village greens.

Many of the cases on user as of right have been decided with reference to town and village greens.[102]

Without interruption

'Without interruption' means some actual and physical stopping of the enjoyment.[103] Use was interrupted where a gate across a path was locked, even though people continued to use the route by going around the side of the gate.[104] Merely challenging the right of the public is not enough. 'Without interruption' does not mean that the public must use the route continuously. In other words, it does not refer to the activity of the user,

---

99 For example, across a village green being contrary to Inclosure Act 1857, s 12 or Commons Act 1876, s 29.

100 *Attorney General (ex rel Yorkshire Derwent Trust) v Brotherton* [1992] 1 AC 425.

101 [2012] EWHC 1976 (Admin).

102 See for instance *R (Lewis) v Redcar and Cleveland Borough Council* [2010] UKSC 11; *Betterment Properties (Weymouth Ltd) v Dorset County Council* [2010] EWHC 3045 (Ch); *R (Oxfordshire & Buckingham Mental Health NHS) v Oxfordshire County Council* [2010] EWHC 530 (Admin); *Barkas v North Yorkshire and Scarborough Council* [2012] EWCA Civ 1373.

103 *Merstham Manor v Coulsdon and Purley UDC* [1937] 2 KB 77.

104 *R v Secretary of State for the Environment ex parte Blake* [1984] JPL 101.

but of the landowner. It has been held that 'use or non use is a question of fact: the cause of any non-use is not the issue'.[105]

When establishing lack of intention to dedicate, any barriers must have been put up with the aim of preventing public access. There does not have to be such an intention where the use of the way is interrupted, but it will be a relevant factor, as will the extent of the interruption. This was explained by the judge in *Fernlee Estates Ltd v City and County of Swansea and National Assembly for Wales*:[106]

> In order to constitute an interruption for the purposes of Section 31 (1) of the Highways Act 1980 there must be some physical and actual interruption which prevents enjoyment of the way rather than merely acts which challenge the user while allowing it to go on: *Merstham Manor Ltd v Coulsdon and Purley* [1937] 2 KB 77, 84–85. A mere absence of continuity in the de facto user will not stop time running, there must be interference with the enjoyment of a right of passage, *Jones v Bates* [1938] 2 All ER 237, 246. Thirdly, 'interruption' means 'interruption of fact'. However, the circumstances of and the intention with which the barring of the way takes place are relevant. For example, the blocking of a road by a broken down vehicle would not amount to a relevant interruption. *Lewis v Thomas* [1950] 1 KB 438.

The locking of a door of an alleyway leading to shops and businesses over the Christmas period was held not to amount to a sufficient interruption of the 20-year period, nor could it be taken as an intention by the landowner not to dedicate a public right of way.[107]

The 20 years' use is not a free standing period. The HA 1980[108] provides, 'The period of 20 years … is to be calculated retrospectively from the date when the right of the public to use the way is brought into question, whether by a notice … or otherwise'. It has been held that the 20-year period can begin and end before the Rights of Way Act 1932, which first introduced this provision, came into force.[109]

The period must, however, end at the time when the right of way is brought into question. It may be brought into question by physical obstructions such as a locked gate, by notices inconsistent with the dedication of a right of way or by stopping people using the path. Court actions for trespass or declarations would also bring the right of way into

---

105 *R (Roxlena) v Cumbria County Council* [2017] EWHC 2651 (Admin).

106 [2001] EWHC 360 (Admin), [16].

107 *Ali v Secretary of State for Environment, Food and Rural Affairs* [2015] EWHC 893 (Admin).

108 HA 1980, s 31(2).

109 *Fairey v Southampton County Council* [1956] 2 QB 439.

question. However, in *Owen v Buckinghamshire County Council*,[110] it was held that the ploughing up of a path was not sufficient.

An application under section 53(5) of the WLCA 1981 for a modification order to show the right on the definitive map and statement would bring the right of way into question. The date is treated as the date on which the application is made under paragraph 1 of Schedule 14 to the WLCA 1981.[111]

This is not an exhaustive list. The essential requirement is that the challenge to the existence of a right of way must be brought home to the public.[112] In *Fairey v Southampton County Council*,[113] it was held that in order to bring into question the right of the public to use a way, a landowner must indicate 'by some means sufficient to bring home to the public that he is challenging their right to use the way, so that they may be apprised of the challenge and have a reasonable opportunity of meeting it'.

The bringing into question does not have to be by the landowner or his agent. It can be by a third party.[114]

There may be several dates when the way is brought into question. Those claiming a right of way will succeed if they can show an interrupted use for 20 years, ending on one of those dates.

Section 31 of the HA 1980 does not state that a public right of way comes into existence after 20 years' use. As explained above, the requirement is that the user must be for 20 years before the right of way is brought into question. Until that time, there is no statutory dedication, however long the user. The right remains merely inchoate until that time. Indeed, until the question has been resolved, either by confirmation of the definitive map order or court action, the right cannot be finally established.

The same argument applies where claims are made for a private right of way under the Prescription Act 1832. The right has to be established by action, and the 20 years must be 'next before suit or action'.[115]

---

110 *Owen v Buckinghamshire County Council* (1957) 55 LGR 373.

111 NERCA 2006, s 69.

112 This has now been held also to be a requirement for a landowner's evidence of lack of intention to dedicate. *R (Godmanchester Town Council) v Secretary of State for Food the Environment and Rural Affairs* [2007] UKHL 28.

113 [1956] 2 QB 439.

114 *Applegarth v Secretary of State for Environment, Transport and Regions* [2001] EWHC 487 (Admin); *R (Godmanchester Town Council) v Secretary of State for Food the Environment and Rural Affairs* [2007] UKHL 28.

115 See Charles Harpum, Stuart Bridge and Martin Dixon (eds), *Megarry and Wade: Law of Real Property* (8th edn, Sweet & Maxwell, 2012), page 1313, para 28–069.

In *De Rothschild v Buckinghamshire County Council*,[116] the public used a path across the De Rothschilds' land for 26 years from 1914 to 1940. The land was requisitioned, and, during that time, there was no evidence of public use. The public's right of way was challenged in 1948, but a claim to a public right of way failed because there had been no use during the 20 years immediately preceding 1948.

This principle has important implications where, for example, vehicular use is claimed over a footpath. If the right of way were brought into question, say, in 2018, 20 years' use before that date could not be established. This is because Part 6 of the NERCA 2006 has prevented any use by a mechanically propelled vehicle after 2 May 2006 from giving rise in the future to any kind of public right of way. Moreover, with limited exceptions, rights which have arisen post-December 1930 but are unrecorded on 2 May 2006 are extinguished. Although it might be possible to establish 20 years' vehicular user before 1930, that would not make the user after that date legal. This is because no right is established until the right of way is brought into question. Any claim based on long use would have to be established at common law, not on statutory deemed dedication, unless it could be shown that the right was called into question before 1930.

3.6.3 The effect of section 31(1) of the Highways Act 1980

The statutory presumption will preclude any argument that the user was attributable to tolerance. In addition, it may, in some situations, counter any argument that the landowner, lacking capacity, could not have dedicated a public right of way.

Where section 31 of the HA 1980 applies, it will be no argument against dedication that, at the time of the deemed dedication, the property was subject to a strict settlement or a trust for sale. This is reinforced by section 33, which enables reversioners under settlements and trusts to bring actions for trespass and injunctions to prevent the acquisition by the public of rights of way as if they were in possession of the land.

The provision enabling a landlord to rebut deemed dedication by placing a notice on that land will also make it difficult for a landlord to allege that there has not been a statutory deemed dedication.

---

116 (1957) 55 LGR 595.

The position of public bodies is specifically left unaltered. Section 31(8) provides:

> Nothing in this section affects any incapacity of a corporation or other body or person in possession of land for public and statutory purposes to dedicate a way over land as a highway if the existence of a highway would be incompatible with those purposes.

The statutory presumption does not apply to the Crown, as public Acts of Parliament do not bind the Crown unless there is a provision to the contrary.

3.7 Limited dedication

3.7.1 General principles

A landowner may dedicate a public right of way subject to physical obstructions such as gates, or the right to plough. The practical difficulty may be in establishing whether the obstruction pre- or post-dated the dedication.

Even where the right of way was originally dedicated subject to a limitation, use of the way for 20 years after the removal of the limitation may amount to re-dedication without the obstruction. So, if a highway was dedicated subject to gates, but the gates were subsequently removed, then after 20 years there would be an unlimited dedication. In *Gloucestershire County Council v Farrow*,[117] it was held that the lord of the manor had lost his right to obstruct the highway with market stalls after he had failed to do so for a period of over 20 years.

The dedication may also be subject to the rights of the landowner, or third parties, to carry on activities on land adjacent to the path which would otherwise amount to a nuisance. A farmer may have dedicated a path subject to his right to plough or carry on other agricultural activities. However, the limitations must not be incompatible with the existence of a right of way. They should, moreover, be entered on the statement attached to the definitive map. If they are not, it will be more difficult for the landowner to prove the limited dedication.

It is assumed that where a landowner dedicates a public right of way, that dedication is subject to his right to use the path for his own purposes. For example, although it is an offence for a member of the public to use a motor vehicle on a footpath or bridleway, a landowner could do so by virtue of his ownership. If the path is publicly maintainable, the legal

---

117 [1985] 1 WLR 741.

analysis is that an easement is reserved over the surface, the legal estate of which is vested in the local authority. An alternative view is that as the vesting in the highway authority is for highway purposes only, the landowner has a concurrent fee simple in the surface.

It seems that dedication may be for limited purposes. In *Winch v Thames Conservators*,[118] it was stated:

> [W]e see no objection to the dedication to the public for … a limited purpose: and in *Severn and Wye Navigation* Holroyd J and Bayley J both laid it down, and we think correctly, that a towing path may be a highway, to be used only for the purpose of towing barges or vessels.

In *Marquis of Stafford v Coyney*,[119] there was a purported dedication of a highway subject to a restriction that wagons carrying coal should be excluded. When a driver of a coal wagon broke down a chain preventing access to the road, Lord Stafford sued in trespass. He succeeded on the basis that there was either a valid partial dedication or no dedication at all.

3.7.2 Restricted byways

The CROWA 2000[120] converted routes which were shown on the definitive map as RUPPs into restricted byways. Restricted byways are subject to any conditions or limitations which existed immediately before the section creating restricted byways came into force.[121]

The Act also provides that any owner or lessee of premises adjoining or adjacent to a restricted byway will, so far as is necessary for the reasonable enjoyment and occupation of the premises, have vehicular access over the relevant highway. 'Relevant highway' means a highway which became maintainable at public expense on the automatic reclassification of a RUPP as a restricted byway and which had previously been owned by the owner, or included in a lease of the premises.

---

118 (1872) LR 7 CP 458; affd (1874) LR 9 CP 378.

119 (1872) 7 B&C 257.

120 CROWA 2000, s 47, which came into force on 2 May 2006: Countryside and Rights of Way Act 2000 (Commencement No 11 and Savings) Order 2006 (SI 2006/1172). See also Restricted Byways (Application and Consequential Amendment of Provisions) Regulations 2006 (SI 2006/1177).

121 CROWA 2000, s 50.

3.8 Private and public rights

It is possible for private and public rights to exist over the same route.[122] For instance, the public may have a right on foot, and a third party may have a private right of way, or easement, for use with vehicles.

If there is a public right of way for vehicles, the landowner will not be able to grant any private vehicular rights because he will have parted with his interest. However, private vehicular rights may have pre-dated the public right, and, should the public rights be extinguished, the person entitled to the benefit of the easement will continue to be able to use the route.

Private vehicular rights may be expressly or impliedly granted or reserved by a landowner. Such a grant may have pre-dated the public dedication or, if the public right is limited to pedestrian or horse use, be granted afterwards provided it does not derogate from the public right already granted.

---

[122] *Applegarth v Secretary of State for Environment, Transport and Regions* [2001] EWHC 487 (Admin); *Parker v Nottinghamshire County Council and the Secretary of State for Food, the Environment and Rural Affairs* [2009] EWHC 229 (Admin).

4 Purchaser

4.1 Introduction

It is obviously important for purchasers and their professional advisers to discover if there are any rights of way, or claims to rights of way, across the property they are going to buy. Rights of way may affect the use, or potential use, of the property. The definitive map is the starting point, but further inquiries should be made, as there may be additional rights or rights of a higher status which are not recorded.

4.2 The definitive map and statement

4.2.1 Inspection of the definitive map

The definitive map and statement is a record maintained by the surveying authority of the public rights of way within its area. It should be available for inspection free of all charge at all reasonable hours.[1]

The district council should also have a copy of that part of the definitive map which covers that district and any orders which have been made amending the map and statement.

Town and parish councils will normally have a copy of that part of the map and statement which covers their parish.

Due to the small scale of the definitive maps, there may be difficulties of interpretation.

4.2.2 Limitations of the definitive map

The definitive map and statement is conclusive as to what is recorded. However, as explained above, there may be perfectly valid rights of way which are not recorded.

There may, for instance, be:

(1) public path orders confirmed but not yet recorded on the definitive map;

---

1 WLCA 1981, s 57.

(2) definitive map orders and public path orders made, but not confirmed;

(3) applications for definitive map or public path orders;

(4) documentary evidence of the valid existence of public rights of way; or

(5) user evidence which would support a claim although no application has yet been made.

Given the scale of most definitive maps, the route on the ground may not be shown with sufficient accuracy. The statement accompanying the map may describe physical features which will identify the position more accurately. Sometimes the statement will give the legal width. However, care must be taken in interpreting the statement. A description of a path in the statement may be giving a legal width or may be just describing the physical feature.

Sometimes there is a conflict between the map and statement. The position was discussed at length in *R (Norfolk County Council) v Secretary of State for the Environment, Food and Rural Affairs*.[2] The judge concluded that if the map and statement cannot be reconciled so that there is a real conflict, the map will prevail. However, if there is an application for a modification order, it all depends on the evidence. There is no presumption that the map is correct and the statement incorrect.

4.3 Enquiries of local authority

The purchaser, or his solicitor, should make enquires on Law Society form Con 29 Enquiries of the Local Authority (2016). This includes questions relating to roads and public rights of way:

> **Roadways footways and footpaths**
>
> 2.1. Which of the roads, footways and footpaths named in the application for this search... are:
>
> (a) highways maintainable at public expense
>
> (b) subject to adoption, and supported by a bond or bond waiver
>
> (c) to be made up by a local authority who will reclaim the cost from the frontagers
>
> (d) to be made up by a local authority without reclaiming the cost from frontagers

---

2 [2005] EWHC 119 (Admin), [38], [64] and [73].

Public rights of way

2.2. Is any public right of way which abuts on, or crosses the property, shown on a definitive map or revised definitive map?

2.3. Are there any pending applications to record a public right of way that abuts, or crosses the property on a definitive map or revised definitive map?

2.4. Are there any legal orders to stop up, divert, alter or create a public right of way which abuts or crosses the property not yet implemented or shown on the definitive map?

2.5. If so please attach a plan showing the approximate route.

The CROWA 2000 introduced a new duty on surveying authorities to keep a register with prescribed information on applications for modification orders to the definitive map.[3] The register aims to increase knowledge among landowners, users of rights of way and the general public about applications which could result in changes to the definitive map and statement. It will also help to avoid duplication of work where someone has already made an application for a definitive map modification order in respect of a particular matter.

However, under the DA 2015, the Secretary of State may, by regulations, provide that applications, made to an authority in England, which do not satisfy the preliminary assessment procedure do not have to be entered on the register.[4] This reduces the burden on the surveying authority, but such regulations will not preclude the authority from including on the register any information which it would be required to include had the regulation not been made.

4.4 Enquiries of the seller

When making preliminary enquiries before contracts are exchanged, the buyer's solicitor should ask whether the seller has any knowledge of public

---

3 CROWA 2000, s 51 and Sch 5, para 2, introducing s 53B into the WLCA 1981. Brought into force in England on 27 September 2005 by the Countryside and Rights of Way Act 2000 (Commencement No 9) Order 2005 (SI 2005/2459) and in Wales on 11 May 2006 by the Countryside and Rights of Way Act 2000 (Commencement No 8 and Transitional Provisions) (Wales) Order 2006 (SI 2006/1279) (W124). The regulations are the Public Rights of Way (Register of Applications under section 53(5) of the Wildlife and Countryside Act 1981) (England) Regulations 2005 (SI 2005/2461); the Public Rights of Way (Registers) (Wales) Regulations 2006 (SI 2006/42) (W8).

4 DA 2015, Sch 7 inserts new subsections (4A) and (4B) into WLCA 1981, s 53B (not yet in force). See Chapter 8 for the preliminary assessment procedure.

rights of way being claimed which do not appear on the definitive map. An incorrect answer may give rise to an action for misrepresentation.[5]

4.5 Inspection of the site

The buyer should inspect the site for any evidence that tracks on the land are being used by the public.

4.6 Title deeds

A landowner's title deeds may show the existence of public rights of way. The grant or reservation of private rights of way may indicate that at that time there was not considered to be a public right of way. However, in most cases title deeds will not reveal any evidence of public rights of way. The fact that the deeds are silent cannot be taken to mean that the rights do not exist.

Where the title is registered, a buyer will take the property subject to overriding interests, whether or not he knows of them. These include public rights of way, but not an adoption agreement under section 38 of the HA 1980.[6]

Where the highway is publicly maintainable, the surface vests in the highway authority, even where the road or path is expressly included in the registered title.[7]

4.7 Inspection of other documentary evidence

In some purchases, the existence of a public right of way, or a right of way of a higher status, may be so detrimental to a prospective buyer that he may employ a solicitor or other professional to investigate documentary records. This process would not normally be undertaken by a solicitor when instructed to act for a buyer.

---

5 *Dart v Ely* [2000] EWCA Civ 259.

6 *Overseas Investment Services Ltd v Simcobuild* (1995) 70 P&CR 322.

7 *Secretary of State for the Environment, Transport and the Regions v Baylis (Gloucester) Ltd* [2000] EGLR 92. Land Registration Rules 1925 (SR&O 1925/1093) (the general boundaries rule), rule 278 did not divest the highway authority of its interest in the surface. The rule is now in Land Registration Act 2002, s 60.

5 Landowner, Tenant and Occupier

5.1 Introduction

Owners and occupiers of land crossed by a public right of way must keep the route visible and not obstruct or endanger users.[1] It is therefore important that they should be aware of any public rights of way over their land. Local authorities (National Park authorities, county councils, some district councils, metropolitan boroughs or unitary authorities) will normally have a 'definitive map' of the area showing public rights of way. These maps are a legal record of public rights of way,[2] showing footpaths, bridleways, restricted byways and BOATs.

5.2 Legal interest in public rights of way

5.2.1 Publicly maintainable highways

Where the public right of way is publicly maintainable, the surface is vested in the highway authority for highway purposes. The landowner is deemed to have a concurrent fee simple, which enables him to use the right of way for his own purposes provided they do not interfere with the rights of public or disturb the surface of the road or path. Where public rights of way are concerned, the landowner usually retains an interest in the subsoil. He also owns the airspace above the highway. This enables him, with the consent of the highway authority, to build cellars or tunnels under the road, or where he owns property on both sides, a building or bridge over the road.

Landowners do not own the subsoil under many major roads. Often, the highway authority will have purchased the land on which the road is built either by a compulsory purchase order or agreement.

---

1 See Natural England Guidance, 'Public rights of way: landowner responsibilities', available at www.gov.uk/guidance/public-rights-of-way-landowner-responsibilities.

2 See Chapter 8.

Adjoining landowners have, subject to planning control, a right of access to the highway from any point of their land[3] and may do repairs to their property from the highway.[4]

5.2.2 Non-publicly maintainable highways

The landowner retains the entire legal interest in the land, but it is subject to the right of passage of members of the public and the rights of control vested in the highway authority.

5.2.3 Statutory restrictions

Although the landowner retains title to the land, his use of the land over which the highway runs may be restricted. For example, without the consent of the highway authority, he may not construct buildings over or under the highway.[5]

5.2.4 The presumption *usque ad medium filum*

Where a right of way separates land in different ownership, there is a presumption that the adjoining landowner owns the land up to the centre point of the track adjoining his property (*usque ad medium filum*).[6] The presumption extends to any waste land between the adjoining land and the highway.[7] The rebuttable presumption that a sale of land adjacent to a highway carries with it that part of the highway which adjoins the land sold is capable of applying to the whole of the highway in question.[8]

This presumption may be rebutted by evidence that ownership of the soil of the track is vested in one adjoining landowner alone or in a third party. However, it will not be rebutted where there is a description in a conveyance that the property is bounded by a road, nor where the property is described by reference to red edging on a plan and the plan does not include the road.[9]

Whether the presumption applies to highways set out under inclosure awards depends on the construction of the award. The presumption rests

---

3 *Lyon v Fishmongers' Co* (1876) 1 App Cas 662.

4 *Cobb v Saxby* [1914] 3 KB 822.

5 HA 1980, ss 176–179.

6 *Central London Railway Co v City of London Land Tax Comrs* [1911] 2 Ch 467.

7 *Steel v Prickett* (1819) 2 Stark 463; *Doe d' Pring v Pearsey* [1824–34] All ER Rep 164.

8 (1) *Commission for New Towns (2) Worcestershire County Council v JJ Gallagher Ltd* [2002] EWHC 2668 (Ch).

9 *Micklethwait v Newlay Bridge Co* (1886) 33 ChD 133.

on the argument that each of the adjoining owners contributed land to the formation of the highway. Where it is a new road, this argument would not be relevant. It may be that the road would remain vested in the lord of the manor unless he was compensated for loss of his rights in the soil.[10]

In new developments, roads are often retained by the developer and do not pass with a sale of the plots. The developers will make up the road to an agreed standard, and the highway authority will adopt the road.

5.2.5 Reservation of implied rights

It is generally accepted that, where a landowner dedicates a public right of way, that dedication is limited to granting the public a right of passage. The landowner is therefore able to use the land over which the right of way exists for his own purposes and to grant others rights insofar as those uses do not derogate from the dedication. Where the public right of way is publicly maintainable so that the surface vests in the highway authority for highway purposes, the landowner will have a concurrent interest in the fee simple.

5.2.6 Adverse possession

It is not possible to acquire title to a highway maintainable at public expense by adverse possession.[11] This is because the surface is vested by statute in the highway authority.[12] Moreover, it is a criminal offence to obstruct a highway.[13]

It is possible that title could be obtained by adverse possession to a highway which is not publicly maintainable.[14] However, the land would be subject to the right of the public to pass and repass over the whole area.

5.2.7 Effect of extinguishment of right of way

The nature of the public's interest in a publicly maintainable right of way is a determinable fee simple. So, if the highway is extinguished, the highway authority's legal interest comes to an end, and the landowner has the fee simple in the surface which is no longer subject to a right of passage.

---

10 *Neaverson v Peterborough RC* [1901] Ch 22.

11 *R (Smith) v Land Registry (Peterborough)* [2010] EWCA Civ 200.

12 Under HA 1980, s 263.

13 HA 1980, s 137.

14 See *R (Smith) v Land Registry (Peterborough)* [2010] EWCA Civ 200, [56] and [57].

5.2.8 The cut-off date

Sections 53 to 56 of the CROWA 2000 provide for the extinguishment on 1 January 2026, subject to certain exceptions, of unrecorded rights of way created before 1949. If the extinguished public right of way was reasonably necessary for a landowner to access his land, it will be converted into a private right of way. It does not matter whether the person was using the existing public right of way on the cut-off date or is able to use it.[15]

5.3 Claims to new rights of way by user

As explained in Chapter 3, new rights of way may arise from user under either common law or section 31 of the HA 1980. In order to rebut any inferred or deemed dedication, the landowner should erect notices indicating that there is no right of way and lodge a statement and declaration under section 31(6). These provisions are discussed in more detail at 3.5.4.

5.4 Maintenance responsibilities

Ascertaining who is liable for the maintenance of a highway is complex. It may be that nobody is liable to do repairs. An example is where a public right of way has been dedicated without following the procedural formalities set out in section 37 of the HA 1980. Another example is where there has been a deemed dedication after 16 December 1949, and no formal public path agreement or order has been entered into.

A landowner may be liable under a local or private Act of Parliament, or, more rarely, liability may have arisen by prescription (liability must have existed from time immemorial), *ratione tenure* (a pre-1290 liability arising from a grant of land in return for an undertaking to do repairs) or enclosure (where a landowner enclosed land so that it was impossible for a traveller to deviate if the route became impassable).

In general, the highway authority is liable for repairs, and it is for the authority to prove otherwise.[16] With regard to public rights of way, many highway authorities take the view that it is less expensive to assume that they are publicly maintainable than to do the necessary research.

---

15 CROWA 2000, s 56.

16 *Attorney General v Watford Rural District Council* [1912] 1 Ch 417.

5.5 Obstructions

5.5.1 What is an obstruction?

An obstruction is 'anything which substantially prevents the public from having free access over the whole of the highway which is not purely temporary in nature'.[17]

In *Herrick v Kidner and Somerset County Council*, Cranston J, having reviewed the case law, said:[18]

> In my view these authorities establish a number of principles with regard to an obstruction of the highway: first, members of the public are in general entitled to unrestricted access to the whole and each part of a highway; secondly, their right to such access is principally to pass and repass but it is also to enjoy other amenity rights; thirdly, those other amenity rights must be reasonable and usual and will depend on the particular circumstances; fourthly, any encroachment upon the highway which prevents members of the public from the enjoyment of these access and amenity rights is an unlawful obstruction; fifthly, the law ignores *de minimis*, or fractional obstructions; and sixthly, a highway authority cannot deprive itself of the power to act against an unlawful obstruction by refraining from exercising its statutory powers against it, or by purporting to give it consent.

Under section 137, a person who, without lawful authority or excuse, wilfully obstructs a highway is guilty of an offence and is liable to pay a fine. The CROWA 2000 has introduced an additional remedy.[19]

A magistrates' court may, on the conviction of a person for wilful obstruction of the highway, order that person to remove the obstruction, provided it is in that person's power to do so. This may be additional to, or instead of, a fine. The order must stipulate what steps are required to remove the obstruction and the timescale within which it must be done. The time allowed by the order may be extended on an application made before the time runs out.

Failure to comply without reasonable excuse with an order to remove an obstruction is an offence punishable by a fine up to level 5 on the standard scale. If the offence is continued, the convicted person is guilty of a further offence and is liable to a fine not exceeding one-twentieth of that level for each day on which the offence is continued. No offence, or further offence,

---

17 *Seekings v Clarke* (1961) 59 LGR 268, 269.

18 [2010] EWHC 269 (Admin), [33].

19 CROWA 2000, s 64, inserting s 137ZA into the HA 1980.

is committed during any time given by the court to the person against whom the order has been made to effect the removal.

Where a person has been convicted for failure to remove an obstruction and the highway authority removes the obstruction, the authority can claim from that person its expenses in doing so.

The Highways (Obstruction by Body Corporate) Act 2004 applies section 314 of the HA 1980 to sections 137 and 137A. Section 314 of the HA 1980 provides that a director, manager, secretary or other similar officer of a body corporate that has committed particular offences under the HA 1980 will be guilty of those offences (as well as the body corporate) if it can be proved that the offence was committed with the consent or connivance of that officer or is attributable to the neglect of the officer.

5.5.2 Overhanging vegetation

Vegetation which overhangs the sides of a path may obstruct the passage of vehicles or pedestrians or endanger or obstruct the passage of horse riders. Where it does so, the highway authority may serve a notice on the owner of the tree, shrub or hedge, or on the occupier of the land on which it is growing, to cut back or lop the vegetation so as to remove the cause of danger, obstruction or interference.[20] Any person aggrieved by the notice may appeal to the magistrates' court. If the works are not carried out in accordance with the notice, the authority can do the work itself and recover the expenses. This power is available whether the vegetation has grown naturally or was deliberately planted.

Where the vegetation grows naturally, it seems no offence of wilful obstruction will have been committed.

5.5.3 Stiles, gates, cattle grids,[21] fences and wires

Gates and other structures across a public right of way amount to an obstruction unless the path was originally dedicated subject to them. The statement accompanying the definitive map should record any limitation on the dedication. On looking at the statement, care should be taken to distinguish between a mere description of the route with obstructions and a dedication which is specifically limited by the obstructions.

If a way has not been dedicated subject to gates or stiles, a statutory notice may be served on the occupier requiring him to remove the structure.[22] If

---

20 HA 1980, s 154, as amended by CROWA 2000, s 65.

21 *Kind v Northumberland County Council* [2012] EWHC 603 (Admin).

22 HA 1980, s 143.

he fails to do so, the authority may remove it and recover its reasonable expenses. In addition, the highway authority may prosecute for obstruction.[23]

Gates in carriageways and bridleways are required to be of a minimum width. For a bridleway, the minimum width is 5 feet; for a carriageway, including a BOAT, the minimum width is 10 feet, measured between the posts. Where the gate is less than the minimum width, the highway authority may, by notice to the owner of the gate, require him to enlarge it to that width or remove it. Failure to do so within 21 days of service of the notice is an offence.[24]

In limited circumstances, the highway authority may give permission to an owner, lessee or occupier for the erection on footpaths or bridleways, and in England on restricted byways and BOATs, of a gate, stile or other structure[25] to prevent the ingress or egress of animals on land which is used, or is being brought into use, for agriculture or forestry or for the breeding and keeping of horses.[26] The authority has no power to authorise gates or stiles for other purposes, such as security. Conditions may be imposed on the size and type of barrier.

In exercising its powers, the authority must have regard to the needs of those with mobility problems. The Secretary of State has the power to issue guidance on the matters which must be taken into account when the authority exercises its power to authorise stiles, gates and other works.

The maintenance of a stile, gate or other structure is the responsibility of the landowner, subject to a contribution of not less than one-quarter of any expenses from the highway authority.[27]

If a landowner does not maintain a stile, gate or similar structure in a safe condition and to the standard of repair required to prevent unreasonable interference with the rights of the persons using the footpath, bridleway, restricted byway or BOAT, the highway authority or district council, after giving 14 days' notice, may enter and do the work and recover the whole of the cost.[28]

---

23 HA 1980, s 137.

24 HA 1980, s 145.

25 This has been held to include cattle grids *Kind v Northumberland County Council* [2012] EWHC 603 (Admin).

26 HA 1980, s 147, as amended by CROWA 2000, s 69 extended to restricted byways and BOATs by DA 2015, s 24 (not yet in force).

27 HA 1980, s 146. This section covers byways; Restricted Byways (Application and Consequential Amendment of Provisions) Regulations 2006 (SI 2006/1177). DA 2015, s 24.

28 HA 1980, s 146(2).

The maintenance liability may be imposed on either the highway authority or the district council under an agreement made with the landowner.

Where a gate or stile has been erected under section 147 or section 147ZA, the maintenance responsibilities will be in accordance with the conditions imposed by the authorisation.

The CROWA 2000 introduced a new section into the HA 1980[29] covering agreements made between the owner, lessee or occupier and the highway authority or district council relating to improvements for the benefit of those with mobility problems. There is provision for the owner, lessee or occupier to do the work in return for payment or part payment of the costs by the competent authority. Alternatively, the agreement could be for the authority to do the work and the owner, lessee or occupier to make the payments. The agreement may contain such conditions as the competent authority thinks fit. These could include conditions as to the maintenance of the structure and for ensuring that the right of way could be exercised without undue inconvenience to the public. Any conditions imposed will replace any previous conditions which existed when the path was created or which were entered into when an authorisation for a structure was granted under section 147 of the HA 1980. The previous conditions or authorisations will cease to have effect 12 months from the date of the agreement or on such earlier date as is specified in the agreement. If there is non-compliance with any condition, the structure will cease to be authorised and the competent authority may, by notice, require its removal.

Fences across a path, unless authorised, will be an obstruction. Electric or barbed wire fences along the side of the path may amount to a public nuisance. If members of the public using the path are likely to wander into the fence, bearing in mind that the path may be used at night, the fence will amount to a nuisance.[30]

As well as being a nuisance at common law, a barbed wire fence can be the subject of a statutory notice under the HA 1980.[31] The occupier of the land may be required to remove the fence within a specified time, and, if he fails to do so, a complaint may be made to a magistrates' court for the making of an abatement order. If the order is not complied with, the authority may do the work in default and recover the expenses.

---

29 HA 1980, s 147ZA, introduced by CROWA 2000, s 69. See also HA 1980, s 175A.

30 *Stewart v Wright* (1893) 9 TLR 480.

31 HA 1980, s 164.

It is an offence under the HA 1980[32] to place a rope or wire across a highway in such a way as to cause danger to a user of the highway. This is sometimes done on public paths temporarily to control stock, but it can be dangerous to horse riders, pedestrians and farm traffic which may have a private right of way along the track.

5.5.4 Ploughing and other disturbances

Ploughing a public right of way is an interference amounting to a public nuisance at common law.

It is possible that a right of way may have been dedicated subject to the right to plough.[33] If this right is recorded in a statement accompanying the definitive map, it is conclusive evidence of its existence. Otherwise, the onus is on the farmer to show that he has a common law right to plough. In most circumstances, the farmer would be better advised to rely on his statutory right to plough.

The statutory right to plough or otherwise to disturb the surface of a footpath or bridleway is contained in the HA 1980.[34] The statutory right applies only to cross-field footpaths and bridleways over agricultural land. There is no right to plough field-edge paths. These are defined as footpaths or bridleways that follow the sides or headlands of fields or enclosures.

BOATs may not be ploughed. Whether or not a RUPP could be ploughed depended on whether it had vehicular rights. Until the RUPP was reclassified under the WLCA 1981, it was not clear in many cases what rights existed on the RUPP. The presumption was that it was a bridleway. If it was alleged that there was no right to plough a cross-field RUPP, it had to be proved that vehicular rights existed.

Since 2 May 2006 when section 47 of the CROWA 2000 came into force, RUPPs have automatically become restricted byways. As a restricted byway has vehicular rights, albeit for non-mechanically propelled vehicles, there is no right to plough under section 134 of the HA 1980.

The right to plough or otherwise disturb, in accordance with the rules of good husbandry, the surface of cross-field bridleways and footpaths is permitted only where it is not reasonably convenient to avoid ploughing or disturbing the surface when sowing or cultivating a crop.

---

32 HA 1980, s 162.

33 *Mercer v Woodgate* (1869) LR 5 QB 26.

34 HA 1980, s 134.

After ploughing or other disturbance, the surface must be made good to at least the minimum width, so that it is reasonably convenient to use and the line is apparent on the ground to at least the minimum width. This must be done within 14 days of the first disturbance for the sowing of the crop or of any subsequent disturbance in connection with that crop within 24 hours, unless a longer period has first been agreed in writing by the highway authority. Where an extension is required, an application must be made to the highway authority before the disturbance occurs or within the relevant time. The extension is subject to a maximum of 28 days.

5.5.5 Crops

Crops, other than grass, will be an obstruction if they grow on or overhang the minimum width of any footpath, bridleway or unmade carriageway so as to inconvenience the public or prevent the line being apparent on the ground.[35] Unmade carriageways include BOATs and restricted byways. A crop will be treated as grass only if 'it is of a variety or mixture commonly used for pasture, silage or haymaking, whether or not it is intended for such a use in that case and is not a cereal crop'.

The over-spraying of crops can interfere with the use of a right of way. It can also endanger people and animals and give rise to an offence under the Health and Safety at Work etc. Act 1974.

If the product label states that people and animals should stay out of a treated crop, warning signs should be placed where the paths enter the sprayed area. The signs should state something to the effect of 'Sprayed: Please Keep to the Path'. They should be left in place until it is safe.

Spraying should be stopped if anyone is using a path which crosses or adjoins the field which is being sprayed.

Any herbicides used to deal with vegetation should be applied in accordance with Health and Safety Regulations and any current Health and Safety Executive (HSE) or Defra codes of practice.

5.5.6 Excavations and other operations

There is no automatic right to carry out excavations or engineering operations on a public right of way. Where, however, such works are reasonably necessary for the purposes of agriculture, the occupier may apply to the highway authority for an order allowing him to disturb the surface of a footpath, bridleway or restricted byway for the

35 HA 1980, s 137A.

period specified in the order.[36] The period is limited to a maximum of 3 months.

The highway authority must make the order if it is satisfied that it is practicable temporarily to divert the path in a manner reasonably convenient to users or that the existing path will be or can be made sufficiently convenient whilst the works are undertaken. When a diversion is made onto land not occupied by the applicant, the written consent of the occupier of that land, and any other person whose consent is needed to obtain access to it, must be obtained.

The order may be made subject to conditions for the benefit of users of the path and where there is a diversion, conditions relating to the provision of signposts and other notices, stiles, bridges and gates.

The authority may recover from the applicant expenses in connection with the order.

5.5.7 Minimum width

The minimum widths referred to in 5.5.4 (Ploughing and other disturbances), 5.5.5 (Crops) and 5.5.6 (Excavations and other operations) are as follows:

(1) the width recorded in the statement attached to the definitive map, if there is such a width recorded (and there seldom is); or

(2)

- (a) a footpath: 1 metre for a cross-field path, 1.5 metres for a field-edge path;
- (b) a bridleway: 2 metres for a cross-field path, 3 metres for a field-edge path;

5.5.8 Enforcement powers

If the occupier does not restore within the statutory time limits a path to the minimum width, the highway authority has powers of entry to do the necessary work and recover the cost.[37] The authority must give not less than 24 hours' notice before entering to do the work. No notice is needed if the entry is just for the purpose of obtaining information. The default powers may be exercised up to a maximum width. This is to provide some

---

[36] HA 1980, s 135; Restricted Byways (Application and Consequential Amendment of Provisions) Regulations 2006 (SI 2006/1177).

[37] HA 1980, s 135; Restricted Byways (Application and Consequential Amendment of Provisions) Regulations 2006 (SI 2006/1177).

tolerance for different types of machinery and equipment and is intended to limit disputes about the exact width that has been restored or cleared. The maximum widths are as follows:

(1) the width (if any) recorded in the statement attached to the definitive map, but if there is no such width recorded;

(2)

 (a) a footpath: 1.8 metres for a cross-field path and field-edge path;

 (b) a bridleway: 3 metres for a cross-field path and field-edge path;

 (c) other unsurfaced highways: 5 metres.

Any person can bring a prosecution against the occupier for not complying with the ploughing or disturbance[38] provisions of the HA 1980 or for failing to keep a public right of way clear of crops.[39]

5.6 Misleading notices

It is an offence for any person to place or maintain on or near any footpath, bridleway or restricted byway shown on a definitive map a notice containing any false or misleading statement likely to deter the public from using the way.[40] The offence does not cover misleading signs on or near BOATs. An example of a misleading sign is 'Trespassers Will be Prosecuted'. As trespass, with limited exceptions, is a civil offence and not a crime, this is a false statement. A notice stating 'Beware of the Bull' would be misleading if there was no bull in the field. The highway authority or district council of the area in which the notice is placed are the authorities which can bring prosecutions under this section. The magistrates' court may impose a fine and order the notice to be removed.

5.7 Bulls

There are special provisions in the WLCA 1981 relating to bulls.[41] The general rule is that it is an offence for the occupier of a field crossed by a

---

38 HA 1980, ss 134 and 135.

39 HA 1980, s 137A.

40 National Parks and Access to the Countryside Act 1949 (NPACA 1949), s 57.

41 HA 1980, s 59.

right of way (footpath, bridleway, restricted byway[42] or BOAT) to keep a bull in the field. No offence will be committed if the bull is either less than 10 months old or not a recognised dairy breed and is at large with cows or heifers. Dairy breeds are Ayrshire, British Friesian, British Holstein, Dairy Shorthorn, Guernsey, Jersey and Kerry.

This provision is not wholly satisfactory, as many people are unable to make the distinction between dairy and beef cattle. However, it is a compromise between the farming community and the users.

Even if the bull comes within the exception, there may be liability under the Health and Safety at Work etc. Act 1974. Section 3 places an obligation on employers and self-employed persons not to put at risk the health and safety of persons not in their employment.

Where a bull is to be kept in a field, the HSE insists on a notice warning that a bull is present. It is advisable to state 'Bull in Field' rather than 'Beware of the Bull', as this might be taken as evidence that the owner knew the bull had vicious tendencies. It is important that the notice is removed when the bull is not in the field, as the notice would then be misleading.

5.8 Occupiers' liability

Neither the highway authority nor the landowner is liable under the provisions of the Occupiers' Liability Acts 1957 and 1984 to users of the highway. This is because the public have a legal right to use the public right of way, and neither the authority nor the landowner can exclude them.[43]

Where, however, a landowner or occupier offers the public an alternative route, which is not an official diversion, the public are given a licence to use that route. The public are not using the route as of right. As they enter that part of the land by express or implied permission, they become invitees. Therefore, there is potential liability under the Occupiers' Liability Act 1957.

The position may be the same where, because of an obstruction caused by the landowner, the user deviates onto land in the ownership of the same

---

42 Restricted Byways (Application and Consequential Amendment of Provisions) Regulations 2006 (SI 2006/1177).

43 *Gautret v Egerton* (1867) LR 2 CP 371; *Greenhalgh v British Railways Board* [1969] 2 QB 286. Occupiers' Liability Act 1984, s 1(7).

landowner.[44] This is on the basis that the landowner has given an implied permission for the deviation.

The landowner owes to the invitee a duty of care. The duty is 'to take such care as in all the circumstances of the case is reasonable to see that the visitor will be reasonably safe in using the premises for those purposes for which he is invited or permitted by the occupier to be there'.[45]

5.9 Occupiers' liability in negligence or nuisance

Where an occupier acts in such a way either on the public right of way or on the adjoining land that a person using the route is injured, the occupier may be liable in negligence. The essentials of the tort of negligence are:

(1) a breach of a duty of care owed by the defendant to the claimant;

(2) a causal connection which is not too remote between the breach and the damage suffered by the claimant; and

(3) the foreseeability that such conduct would have inflicted on that claimant the particular kind of damage which he suffered.

In ascertaining the amount of damages for any injury, any contributory negligence of the claimant will be taken into account.

An occupier may be liable in nuisance if he does something which interferes with a member of the public's enjoyment of a right of way. An example would be depositing something on the path, or erecting a wire fence too close to a footpath.

5.10 Diversions or extinguishments

Landowners may find that their farming activities or the development of their land is hindered by public rights of way. It may be possible to have a path diverted or, more rarely, extinguished, under the statutory provisions discussed in Chapter 6.

---

44 *Stacey v Sherrin* (1913) 29 TLR 555.

45 Occupiers' Liability Act 1957, s 2(2).

6 Diversions and Extinguishments

6.1 Introduction

There is a legal adage, 'Once a highway always a highway'.[1] This means that even though a highway has not been used for many years and even though it may not be visible on the ground, it will continue to have legal existence.[2] It also means that it is not possible to establish title by adverse possession to a publicly maintainable highway or to restrict the public's right of passage.[3]

In order for a highway to be extinguished or diverted, there must be an order made under statutory provision. There is an exception where the highway has ceased to exist physically. The obvious example is a footpath along a cliff which is eroded and falls into the sea.[4] It is sometimes difficult to ascertain whether a path running, say, by a river can be repaired or has ceased to exist entirely. In *R v Secretary of State for the Environment, Transport and the Regions ex parte Gloucestershire County Council*,[5] it was held that the erosion of the river bank destroyed the path and did not give a right to deviate inland. On the other hand, where a landslip destroyed a metalled road, it was held that the highway continued to exist along the line of the old road.[6] There is another possible exception where a public right of way is inaccessible. In *Bailey v Jamieson*,[7] a public footpath became inaccessible due to the stopping up of the highway at either end. This was followed in

---

1 See e.g. *R v Inhabitants of St James, Taunton* (1315) Selwyn's NSR; *Harvey v Truro RDC* [1903] 2 Ch 638.

2 *Attorney General v Stokesley RDC* (1928) 26 LGR 440.

3 *Gerring v Barfield* (1864) 16 CB (NS) 597; *R (Smith) v The Land Registry Peterborough* [2010] EWCA Civ 200. See 2.4.

4 *R v The Inhabitants of the Parish of Paul in Cornwall* (1840) 2 Mood and R 307 (wall carrying right of way washed into the sea); *R v The Inhabitants of Hornsea in the East Riding of Yorkshire* (1854) Dears CC 291 (part of road eroded). See, however, the provisions for 'roll back' of the long-distance trail under MCAA 2009, Pt 9. Section 302 of the Act introduces a new s 55B into the NPACA 1949.

5 [2000] EGCS 150.

6 *R v The Inhabitants of Greenhow in the North Riding of Yorkshire* (1876) 1 QBD 703.

7 (1876) 1 CPD 329.

Kumar Shamrao Kotegaonkar v (1) Secretary of State for the Environment, Food & Rural Affairs (2) Bury Metropolitan Borough Council.[8] The court ruled that a footpath linking two privately owned sites, one containing a health centre and the other containing shops, could not be a public highway, either at common law or under section 31 of the HA 1980, because members of the public had no legal right of entry at either end of the path; they entered the health centre and the shops under licence from the respective landowners, not because they had an unrestricted right to do so.

Public rights of way may be stopped up or diverted under public, private or local Acts of Parliament. This chapter deals with the public Acts under which most orders are made.[9]

Copies of orders confirmed or certified (where the order is not to come into effect until the authority has so certified) should be sent to Ordnance Survey.[10]

6.2 Effect of orders

6.2.1 Stopping-up orders

The effect of a stopping-up order is that the right of the public to pass and repass is extinguished. Where the surface of the path is publicly maintainable, the determinable fee simple which was vested in the highway authority will cease.[11] The fee simple will therefore revest in the landowner free of the public rights. However, any private rights will continue.[12]

It is also possible for some, rather than all, of the rights to be extinguished. Vehicular rights could be extinguished, but bridleway and pedestrian rights retained.

6.2.2 Diversion orders

A diversion is an alteration of the route of the path. This usually means that the old route will be closed and a new route created. There is some

---

8 [2012] EWHC 1976 (Admin).

9 Defra, Rights of Way Circular 1/09, 'Guidance for Local Authorities' (Defra, 2009) Ch 5 gives information and advice on public path orders including creation orders.

10 See Defra, Rights of Way Circular 1/09, 'Guidance for Local Authorities' (Defra, 2009) para 5.60 and table.

11 *Tunbridge Wells Corporation v Baird* [1896] AC 434; *Rolls v St George the Martyr Southwark, Vestry* (1880) 14 Ch D 785.

12 *Walsh v Oates* [1953] 1 QB 578.

conflicting case law on whether the diversion needs to be to an entirely or partially new route, or to an existing route which is improved in some way.[13] Much depends on the statutory provision under which the diversion is being made.[14]

6.2.3 Judicial and administrative orders

Historically, highway matters were dealt with at Quarter Sessions. The jurisdiction of the magistrates' court has been retained in relation to a limited number of issues, including the diversion and extinguishment of highways.[15] However, there is also an administrative procedure for extinguishing and diverting restricted byways,[16] bridleways and footpaths,[17] but not vehicular routes for mechanically propelled vehicles.

6.3 Judicial orders

6.3.1 Use of section 116 of the Highways Act 1980

Under this section, orders for stopping up and diversions may be made for all kinds of highways other than trunk roads and special roads. This is in contrast to orders (other than special extinguishment and diversion orders) under sections 118 and 119, which can be made only in relation to footpaths, bridleways and restricted byways. Section 116 can be used to extinguish rights for mechanically propelled vehicles subject to the reservation of a restricted byway, bridleway or footpath rights.[18] It is not possible to use section 118 in this manner so as to preserve lesser rights. However, provided the appropriate tests can be fulfilled, a bridleway could be extinguished and, concurrently, a new right created for walkers.[19]

---

13 *Welch v Nash* (1807) 8 East 394; *De Ponthieu v Pennyfeather* (1814) 5 Taunt 634; *R v Phillips* (1866) LR 1 QB 648. *R (Ramblers Association) v Secretary of State for Defence* [2007] EWHC 1398 (Admin).

14 See S Sauvain, *Highway Law* (5th edn, Sweet & Maxwell, 2013), paras 9-12–9-15. Under TCPA 1990, s 257(2)(a), diversions may be made to existing highways.

15 HA 1980, s 116.

16 Restricted Byways (Application and Consequential Amendment of Provisions) Regulations 2006 (SI 2006/1177).

17 HA 1980, ss 118 and 119.

18 HA 1980, s 116(4), as amended by CROWA 2000, Sch 5, Pt II, para 15. In considering whether any public right of way should be reserved, any access land is to be disregarded, see CROWA 2000, s 59.

19 E.g. under HA 1980, s 26.

Where bridleways and footpaths are concerned, local authorities are encouraged by Defra to use sections 118 and 119 rather than section 116.[20]

6.3.2 Stopping up

A public right of way may be stopped up if it appears to the magistrate that the way is unnecessary. 'Unnecessary' means unnecessary for the public.[21] What is or is not unnecessary depends on the facts in a particular case. Use does not of itself indicate that the highway is necessary, although it will obviously be an important factor to take into account. The existence of an alternative route may be relevant,[22] but access land under the CROWA 2000 is not to be taken into account in considering whether the existing highway is unnecessary or whether any public right of way should be reserved.[23]

Section 116 may be used to reduce the width of a highway.

However, even if the magistrates consider the route unnecessary, they still have a discretion on whether to order that the highway be stopped up.

In *Maile v Manchester City Council*, Laws J said:[24]

> Section 116(1) confers, of course, no more nor less than a discretion in the court to authorise the stopping-up of a highway. The discretion only arises if the Court concludes that the highway is unnecessary. That being the position the court is not, in my judgment, limited to the bare question whether the highway is necessary or not necessary when it comes to exercise the discretion.

According to Ouseley J in *R (Spice) v Leeds City Council*:[25]

> In reaching a decision as to whether a strip of land is unnecessary for the performance of highway functions, of course the starting point is whether or not it is used for passing or re-passing. But it would be a misconstruction of the totality of Highway Act powers to treat that as the exclusive scope of the relevant inquiry. In considering whether the strip was unnecessary, it would be necessary to consider, in the case of land over

---

20 Defra, Rights of Way Circular 1/09, 'Guidance for Local Authorities' (Defra, 2009) para 5.58.

21 *Ramblers' Association v Kent County Council* (1990) 60 P&CR 464, but see *Westley v Hertfordshire County Council* [1995] CL 846: parking not a relevant use of the highway.

22 See unreported case *Stevens v Dorset County Council* (16 March 1999) – use by Trail Riders Fellowship not necessary where 140 miles of unpaved country road including 10 miles of byways in Dorset were available.

23 CROWA 2000, s 59.

24 [1997] EWHC 2948 (Admin), [38].

25 [2006] EWHC 661 (Admin), [40].

> which section 96 powers were exercised, whether it was performing an amenity or other function which required the trees or fences to be there, whether for amenity, verge protection or for some other purpose. It could be necessary for the highway to perform a function in relation to safety or access for third parties. Those, in my judgment, would all fall under the heading of 'unnecessary'.

No compensation is payable for loss suffered by anyone as a result of the stopping up of the highway.

6.3.3 Diversion

In order for a diversion to be made, the new route must be nearer or more commodious for the public. The convenience of the landowner is not relevant. 'Commodious' has been interpreted to mean 'a flavour of convenience, roominess and spaciousness'.[26]

Although it seems that the diversion can be to an existing route[27] if that route is to be extended or enlarged, where there is no such alteration to the route, the proper course would be to apply for a stopping-up order rather than a diversion.

Where a diversion is made, the new route should carry the same rights as the old route.[28] If lesser rights are to be diverted, there must be a stopping-up order for the greater rights. For example, the vehicular rights could be stopped up on a BOAT, and the remaining bridleway and footpath rights diverted.

The consent of the owner of the land, over which the diverted way will run, is required, but there is no provision for compensation.

Where a diversion order is made, it does not take effect until the new route has been completed and a certificate signed by two justices that it has been completed to their satisfaction. Until that is done, the order is not effective.[29]

6.3.4 Cost of application

An individual may request the highway authority to make an application for a stopping-up or diversion order. The authority may require that

---

26 *Gravesham Borough Council v Wilson and Straight* [1983] JPL 607.

27 See 6.2.2, fn 14.

28 *Ramblers' Association v Kent County Council* (1990) 60 P & CR 464.

29 HA 1980, s 116(8); *Stockwell v Southgate Corporation* [1936] 2 All ER 1343.

person to pay the reasonable costs in making the application for the order, as a condition of granting the request.[30]

6.3.5 Procedure

Before making an application by means of a complaint to the magistrates' court, notice of the proposal must be given to the district and parish councils. If, within 2 months of receiving notice, either council refuses in writing its consent to the application, the application cannot go ahead.[31] There is no requirement that consent should not reasonably be withheld, which means that the councils have the power of veto.

Where the application is for a diversion order, the consent of every owner of land over which the route is to run must be obtained and produced to the court.[32]

At least 28 days before the application for an order is made, the application authority must give notice to the owners and occupiers of all the lands which adjoin the highway of its intention to apply for the order specifying the time and place at which the application is to be made and its terms. Notices must also be served on any statutory undertakers with apparatus in, over, along or across the path.[33] In addition, notices embodying the plan must be displayed in prominent positions at the ends and intersections of the path.[34] This is generally taken to mean that the plan should be displayed on the site. However, a reference to a plan which can be inspected at the council's office was upheld in the unreported case of *Stevens v Dorset County Council*.[35]

The notices must specify the time and place for the hearing, the terms of the proposed order, and must also include a plan showing the effect of the order.

The justices must be satisfied before making an order that all the notices have been given and that the consents of the owners over whose land the

---

30 HA 1980, s 117. On the approach to be adopted by a highway authority when deciding a request for a stopping-up order under s 117, see *R (Spice) v Leeds City Council* [2006] EWHC 661 (Admin). The same considerations apply as when a highway authority makes an application under s 116.

31 HA 1980, s 116(3).

32 HA 1980, s 116(8).

33 For the powers and rights of the statutory undertakers, see HA 1980, Sch 12, Pt II.

34 HA 1980, Sch 12. See *Ramblers' Association v Kent County Council* (1990) 60 P&CR 464, on the importance of notices not to be misleading and what amounts to 'ends of the highway'.

35 16 March 1999, Co/2149/98.

diverted highway will run have been lodged with the court. Recipients of the notices, users of the highway and aggrieved persons are entitled to be heard.

The order, accompanied by a plan, when made, must be signed by the chairman and sent to the authority which made the application.

6.3.6 Appeals

A right of appeal to the Crown Court against an order made by the magistrates' court is given to the highway authority or anyone who was or claimed to be entitled to be heard at the magistrates' court.[36]

6.4 Extinguishment orders under section 118 of the Highways Act 1980

6.4.1 The tests

Restricted byways,[37] bridleways and footpaths, but not vehicular routes for mechanically propelled vehicles, may be extinguished under section 118. This is achieved by a two-stage process: first, the making of an order and, secondly, the confirmation. There are separate criteria which must be fulfilled at each stage.

In making the order, it must appear to the county council or local authority[38] '... that it is expedient that the path or way should be stopped up on the ground that it is not needed for public use'.

In deciding this question, the council must not consider any access land under the CROWA 2000 as reducing the need.[39] It must have due regard to the needs of agriculture, forestry and nature conservation.[40]

In confirming the order, the local authority must be satisfied:

> ... that it is expedient to do so having regard to the extent (if any) to which it appears ... that the path or way would, apart from the order, be likely to be used by the public and having regard to the effect which the

---

36 HA 1980, s 317.

37 Restricted Byways (Application and Consequential Amendment of Provisions) Regulations 2006 (SI 2006/1177).

38 'Local authority' means the council of a district or London borough or the Common Council of the City of London, but in relation to Wales, it means a Welsh council: HA 1980, s 329.

39 CROWA 2000, s 59(2).

40 HA 1980, ss 121(3) and 29, as amended by CROWA 2000, Sch 6, Pt I, para 14(4).

extinguishment of the right of way would have as respects the land served by the path or way, account being taken as to the provisions for compensation.

The difference in wording between 'appears' and 'is satisfied' may reflect the difference in procedure. An order is made without a full inquiry into objections. If objections are made, there is a public inquiry, a hearing or written representations that provide an opportunity for the inspector to weigh up the evidence on both sides.

The difference between the test of 'not needed for public use' at the order-making stage and the extent that the path is 'likely to be used by the public' at the confirmation stage is significant. The Secretary of State or local authority may confirm the order even if the path was used to something more than a minimal extent provided it was not needed, because, for instance, there was a convenient alternative path.[41] However, in considering the question of the extent to which the highway is likely to be used, where it is on or near access land, he must have regard to its use at any time when the right of entry to the access land is not exercisable.[42]

The question of need is decided by the order-making authority. That question does not come to the inspector by way of appeal. The inspector, however, in deciding whether it is expedient to confirm the order, can take into account additional considerations as well as use by the public.

When making or confirming an order, any temporary circumstances preventing or diminishing the use of the path by the public are ignored.[43] 'Temporary circumstances' include substantial buildings, such as electricity sub-stations, and trees and high hedges. There is an obvious judicial reluctance to allow highways to be extinguished on the basis that they had previously been improperly obstructed.[44]

In deciding whether to confirm an extinguishment order, the Secretary of State or, where the order is unopposed, the council, must have regard to any improvement plan which includes the area in which the path lies.[45]

---

41 HA 1980, s 118(5). *R v Secretary of State for the Environment ex parte Stewart* [1980] JPL 175; *R v Secretary of State for the Environment ex parte Cheshire County Council* [1991] JPL 537.

42 CROWA 2000, s 59(3).

43 HA 1980, s 118(6).

44 CROWA 2000, s 118(6). *Wood v Secretary of State for the Environment* [1977] JPL 307; *R v Secretary of State for the Environment ex parte Stewart* [1980] JPL 175.

45 HA 1980, s 118(6A), as inserted by CROWA 2000, Sch 6, Pt I, para 6.

In making the order, the authority must have due regard to the needs of agriculture, forestry and nature conservation.[46]

6.4.2 Concurrent orders

Section 118(5) envisages that there will be concurrent orders involving creation and diversion orders and extinguishment orders. In making and confirming an extinguishment order, the local authority or Secretary of State 'may have regard to the extent to which the public path creation order or the public path diversion order would provide an alternative path'. Agreements may also be taken into account, but not where the agreement to create a replacement path is conditional on the confirmation of the extinguishment order.[47]

There is, however, no similar provision which provides that, when deciding whether there is a need for a new footpath or bridleway, extinguishment or diversion orders should be taken into account. From this, it seems that the need test must be satisfied on its own.

If this is right, on a reorganisation of public rights of way, the first question must be whether there is a need for new rights.

In considering whether a path is needed for public use, 'any temporary circumstances preventing or diminishing the use of a path or way by the public' are to be disregarded. Temporary circumstances do not mean temporary structures. Case law has established that some substantial obstructions, such as buildings, have to be disregarded if they could legally and physically be removed.[48]

Concurrent orders may be useful when the tests for a diversion order cannot be satisfied. A creation and an extinguishment order could be made. Another example is where an authority might want to divert two paths onto a single new route. It could extinguish one route and divert the other. As there is no power under section 118 to downgrade a bridleway to a footpath, an extinguishment order could be made and an order made to create a footpath over the same route.

---

46 HA 1980, ss 121(3) and 29, as amended by CROWA 2000, Sch 6, Pt I, para 14(4).

47 *R (Hertfordshire County Council) v Department of Environment, Food & Rural Affairs* [2006] EWCA Civ 1718.

48 *R (Ashbrook) v East Sussex County Council* [2002] EWCA Civ 1701.

6.4.3 Applications relating to agricultural land and other land specified in regulations

Although an owner, lessee or occupier might request an extinguishment order, many local authorities have been reluctant to make orders unless they are concurrent with orders for the creation or diversion of other rights of way. Even if the tests for making and confirming an order are satisfied, the authority is not under a duty to make an order. It may, in exercising its discretion, decide that it is not expedient to do so. There will often be opposition to the closure of paths, and local authorities are therefore sometimes unwilling to use their limited resources to make orders. They are specifically directed not to make orders which result in cul-de-sac paths.[49]

Although there is provision for the Secretary of State to use his reserve powers should a local authority refuse to make an order,[50] these powers are seldom used.

The position of an owner, lessee or occupier of any land used for agriculture, forestry or the breeding or keeping of horses was strengthened by the CROWA 2000, which made prospective amendments to the HA 1980.[51] They were given a formal right of application for an extinguishment order with a right of appeal against the authorities' refusal to make an order. In the event these provisions were not brought into force. In August 2008, Defra announced that it was not going to implement the provisions in their present form and that further primary legislation was required.

The DA 2015 [52] has amended section 118ZA(1) (although this section is not yet in force) so that it reads 'the owner, lessee or occupier of any land used for agriculture, forestry, or the breeding or keeping of horses or of any land of a prescribed description' may apply for an extinguishment order in relation to a footpath or bridleway which crosses the land.

An application has to be made on a prescribed form and be accompanied by a map on a scale which is to be prescribed. The map is required to show the land over which the right of way is to be extinguished.

In Wales, there is power for regulations to prescribe any fees payable for making the application and any further charges if the application is granted. However, the amount of the charges will be set centrally and may not be

---

49 Defra, Rights of Way Circular 1/09, 'Guidance for Local Authorities' (Defra, 2009) para 7.18.

50 HA 1980, s 120(3).

51 HA 1980, s 118ZA; CROWA 2000, Sch 6, Pt I, para 7.

52 DA 2015, s 23 (not yet in force).

sufficient for the authority to recover all its costs. This limitation does not apply in England. Section 150 of the Local Government and Housing Act 1989 enables authorities to authorise charges for applications under sections 118ZA and 119ZA, which would be at the authorities' discretion provided the charges did not exceed the actual costs.

When the new rules come into force in England, the council has to determine the application as soon as reasonably practicable. If the council does not make its decision within 4 months, the applicant can apply to the Secretary of State, who, after consulting with the council, can direct the council to make the order before the end of a specified period.[53]

Before making an order, the council can require the applicant to pay any compensation due to a third party whose land had been depreciated, or who has suffered damage by being disturbed in his enjoyment of land, by the order.[54]

After an application has been determined, the council has to give the applicant notice of the decision with reasons for it, and a copy of the notice has to be given to prescribed persons.

Although the new procedures, if introduced, should mean that orders will be made more readily, it will still be necessary to satisfy the council, or the Secretary of State, that the path is not needed for public use. It will often not be possible to do this.

Where landowners have compelling reasons for wanting a right of way to be extinguished, they will have to give serious consideration to creating new rights of way where the public want them. They may then be able to show that the existing path is not needed. Otherwise, they should concentrate on managing the right of way and seeking other solutions to perceived problems.

6.5 Diversion orders under section 119 of the Highways Act 1980

6.5.1 The tests

Restricted byways,[55] bridleways and footpaths may be diverted under section 119. In the same way as for extinguishments, the procedure for a

---

53 HA 1980, s 118ZA(7), inserted by CROWA 2000, Sch 6, Pt I, para 7. (The government has announced that s 118ZA will not be implemented.)

54 HA 1980, s 118ZA(6).

55 Restricted Byways (Application and Consequential Amendment of Provisions) Regulations 2006 (SI 2006/1177).

diversion is for an order to be made and then confirmed. Where there are objections, the order must be referred to the Secretary of State for confirmation or otherwise, unless the council decides to withdraw the order.[56]

In deciding whether to make an order, the council must consider that it is expedient 'in the interests of the owner, lessee or occupier of land crossed by the path or way or of the public' that the path should be diverted. No limitation is placed on the interests of owners, lessees or occupiers, and diversions can therefore be obtained on grounds of security or privacy.[57]

However, an order must not alter a point of termination if that point is not on a highway. In other words, a highway authority has no power to divert the cul-de-sac end of a route. Where the termination point is on a highway, the diversion must be to another point on the same highway or a highway connected with it and it must be as substantially convenient to the public.[58]

In making the order, the council must have regard to agriculture, forestry and nature conservation.[59]

Unlike extinguishment orders, there is no specific provision for disregarding temporary circumstances preventing or diminishing use, but in practice they will be taken into account.[60]

For an order to be confirmed, the highway authority or the Secretary of State must be satisfied not only that it is expedient in the interests of the owner, lessee or occupier of the land crossed by the path or the public, but also that the diverted path will not be substantially less convenient to the public as a consequence of the diversion. In addition, it must be expedient to confirm the order having regard to[61] the effect the diversion would have on:

---

56 *R (Hargrave) v Stroud District Council* [2002] EWCA Civ 1281.

57 *Robertson v Secretary of State for the Environment* [1976] 1 WLR 371 (diversion of path across the Chequers Estate).

58 HA 1980, s 119(2).

59 HA 1980, ss 121(3) and 29, as amended by CROWA 2000, Sch 6, Pt I, para 14(4). See also HA 1980, s 85(1): special considerations in AONBs.

60 The Planning Inspectorate, Rights of Way Section, Advice Note No 9, 'General guidance on public rights of way matters' (Revised November 2014), para 29, available at www.gov.uk.

61 This is a separate requirement from the provision that the path must not be less convenient to the public as a consequence of the diversion: *R (Young) v Secretary of State for the Environment, Food and Rural Affairs* [2002] EWHC 844 (Admin).

(1) public enjoyment of the path;

(2) other land served by the existing right of way, taking into account the provision for compensation; and

(3) the land over which the new route will pass.[62]

In deciding whether to confirm the order, the material provisions of any improvement plan for the area must be considered.[63]

There are no standard widths for the new paths created by diversion orders. However, a width should be specified in the order.

6.5.2 Diversions onto an existing highway

The new route to which the path is diverted may include part of an existing highway. Section 119(7)(b), which is concerned with maps to be attached to public path diversion orders, states that the map should indicate 'whether a new right of way is created by the order over the whole of the new site or whether some part of it is already comprised in a footpath or bridleway'. Section 119(2)(b), dealing with the requirement that where a route terminates on a highway, the diverted route should terminate on the same highway (or one connected to it), also envisages that the diversion may be to an existing route. If the existing route is of a higher status, the diverted route will take that status.

However, it would not appear that a diversion order could be made to an existing route without any new route being provided.[64] The appropriate order in such circumstances would be an extinguishment order.

6.5.3 Diversions with limitations and conditions

The diversion order may specify that the diverted route be subject to limitations or conditions even if the original route which is extinguished by the order was not so subject.[65] These limitations or conditions should be recorded in the order.

---

62 HA 1980, s 119(6).

63 HA 1980, s 119(6A).

64 *R v Lake District Special Planning Board ex parte Bernstein* (1982) *The Times*, 3 February.

65 HA 1980, s 119(4).

6.5.4 Compensation

Compensation is payable to anyone whose property can be shown to have been adversely affected by public path orders under the HA 1980.[66] For example, compensation could be claimed by a landowner where a path is created over or diverted onto his land. An application should be made in writing to the local authority which made the order, or the authority nominated by the Secretary of State where he made the order, within 6 months of the coming into operation of the order.[67] Disputes as to the amount of compensation are decided by the Upper Tribunal (Lands Chamber).[68] An action to recover the money must be brought within 6 years from the date when the claim for compensation was lodged.[69]

6.4.5 Physical setting out of the path

Works may be necessary to create the new path on the diverted route. Until such time as the highway authority certifies that the work has been done, the old route will continue to exist.[70]

6.6.6 The practicalities

There are differing perceptions about the making and confirmation of diversion orders. Landowners consider that applications for diversions are very rarely successful, whilst ramblers have statistics to prove that diversion orders are usually confirmed.

What is clear is that much homework is necessary before an application is made. A person who wants a diversion should make sure that the diversion achieves what he wants, fulfils the tests set out in section 119 and gives some extra advantage to the public.

Important considerations include the effect the diversion will have on other paths in the neighbourhood, and whether the new route will be easier to walk, or provide better views.

The applicant should consult all the possible interested parties. These include the landowner, the tenant, the highway authority, the parish council and local user groups.

---

66 HA 1980, ss 121(2) and 28.

67 Public Path Order Regulations 1993 (SI 1993/11), reg 5.

68 HA 1980, ss 307 and 309.

69 Limitation Act 1980, s 9; *Rotherwick v Oxfordshire County Council* (2002) 28 EG 144.

70 HA 1980, s 119(3), as amended by CROWA 2000, Sch 6, Pt I, para 9(3).

Although there is no specific provision that temporary circumstances preventing the use of the existing path should be taken into account when considering a diversion order, local authorities may refuse to make a diversion order if there are obstructions on the original route.[71]

A local authority is not under a duty to make a diversion order[72] and may in its discretion decide not to do so even though the tests under section 119 have been fulfilled. Where an order is not made but an owner, lessee or occupier of land crossed by a footpath or bridleway satisfies the Secretary of State that it is expedient to make a diversion order, the Secretary of State may himself make an order, provided that he has powers to confirm any order so made.[73] He must consult with the appropriate authority before doing so. In practice, these reserve powers are seldom used.

The position of an owner, lessee or occupier of any land used for agriculture, forestry or the breeding or keeping of horses was strengthened by the HA 1980, as amended by the CROWA 2000.[74] They were given a formal right of application for a diversion order with a right of appeal against the authorities' refusal to make an order. However, as explained at 6.3.3, these provisions were not brought into force.

The DA 2015[75] has amended section 119ZA(1) (not yet in force) so that it reads 'the owner, lessee or occupier of any land used for agriculture, forestry, or the breeding or keeping of horses or of any land of a prescribed description' may apply for an diversion order in relation to a footpath or bridleway which crosses the land.

When the relevant provisions are in force, the following provisions will apply. Where the diverted route would link to a classified road, a special road, a Greater London Authority road or any other highway for which the minister is responsible, the consent of the relevant highway authority will be required.[76] The consent of any statutory undertaker will be required where the diverted route will pass over land covered by its works or the curtilage of such land.[77]

---

71 See *R (Ashbrooke) v East Sussex County Council* [2002] EWCA Civ 1701.

72 *R (Hargrave) v Stroud District Council* [2002] EWCA Civ 1281. See Defra, Rights of Way Circular 1/09, 'Guidance for Local Authorities' (Defra, 2009) para 5.29.

73 HA 1980, s 120(3).

74 HA 1980, s 119ZA; CROWA 2000, Sch 6, Pt I, para 7 (not yet in force).

75 DA 2015, s 23 (not yet in force).

76 HA 1980, s 119ZA(2) (not yet in force).

77 HA 1980, s 119ZA(3) (not yet in force).

An application will have to be made on a prescribed form and be accompanied by a map on a scale to be prescribed. The map must show the line of the existing path and the proposed new route. The map must indicate whether it is proposed to create a new right of way over the whole of the new site or whether some of it is already comprised in a footpath or bridleway.[78]

The council must determine the application as soon as reasonably practicable.[79] If the council does not make its decision within 4 months, the applicant may apply to the Secretary of State, who, after consulting with the council, may direct the council to make the order before the end of a specified period.[80]

After an application has been determined, the council must give the applicant notice of the decision with reasons for it, and a copy of the notice must be given to prescribed persons.[81]

6.6 Diversions and extinguishments for planning purposes

6.6.1 General principles

Planning permission is generally needed for development. This is defined as[82] 'The carrying out of building, engineering, mining or other operations in, on, over or under land, or the making of any material change in the use of any buildings or other land'.

Certain classes of development covered by a general or special development order do not require planning permission.

The grant of planning permission, whether outline or full, does not extinguish or divert any existing public rights of way. Nor does it preclude a modification order being made to add additional public rights of way to the definitive map if their legal existence can be proved.

In the past, the existence of a public right of way was often not taken into account on an application for planning permission. However, the Rights

---

78 HA 1980, s 119ZA(4) (not yet in force).

79 HA 1980, s 119ZA(7) (not yet in force).

80 HA 1980, s 119ZA(8) (not yet in force).

81 HA 1980, s 119ZA(9) (not yet in force).

82 TCPA 1990, s 55.

of Way Circular 1/09, 'Guidance for Local Authorities', issued by Defra, states:[83]

> The effect of development on a public right of way is a material consideration in the determination of applications for planning permission and local planning authorities should ensure that the potential consequences are taken into account whenever such applications are considered.

In addition, the Town and Country Planning (General Development Procedure) Order 1995[84] requires that a development affecting a public right of way must be advertised in a local newspaper and by posting a notice on the site.

Once planning permission has been obtained, the developer will need to obtain a diversion or extinguishment order before proceeding with the development. He cannot assume that because he has obtained planning permission, an order will automatically be made and confirmed. It is therefore best if an application for a diversion or stopping-up order is made at the same time as the application for planning permission.[85]

Where there is a confirmed diversion order, it will be for the developer to construct any new path. The highway authority or order-making authority must certify that the diverted path has been constructed to a satisfactory standard. Until that certificate is issued, there is no legal change in the right of way, even though there is a confirmed order.

6.6.2 Order made by the Secretary of State under section 247 of the Town and Country Planning Act 1990

The Secretary of State has powers to authorise by order[86] the stopping up or diversion of any highway (vehicular routes, bridleways, footpaths), if he is satisfied it is necessary to enable development to be carried out in accordance with planning permission or under a general development

---

83 Defra, Rights of Way Circular 1/09, 'Guidance for Local Authorities' (Defra, 2009) para 7.2. See also Department for Communities and Local Government, 'The Validation of Planning Applications – Guidance for local planning authorities' (December 2007) and Department for Communities and Local Government, Circular 02/2008, 'Standard application form and validation' (March 2008).

84 (SI 1995/419).

85 For guidance, see Defra, Rights of Way Circular 1/09, 'Guidance for Local Authorities' (Defra, 2009) Ch 7.

86 The terminology differs. A local authority makes an order, and it is confirmed by the authority or the Secretary of State. The Secretary of State proposes to make an order and then makes (rather than confirms) the order.

order or where permission is not needed (e.g. where the development is by a government department).[87]

A developer who seeks to persuade the Secretary of State to make the order may be required to meet the expenses incurred by the Secretary of State or the highway authority in making alternative routes or paying compensation to third parties.

In England, a draft order for the stopping up or diversion of a highway can be published at the same time as the application for planning permission.[88] In Wales, an application cannot generally be made unless planning permission has first been obtained. The order must be necessary to enable the development to be carried out. The development must therefore not have been completed before the application is made. It can, however, have been begun and have already blocked the highway.[89]

There are exceptions to the rule that planning permission must be obtained before an application is made. Under section 253, the Welsh ministers may make a draft order in anticipation of planning permission where the application for permission is before them on a call-in[90] or appeal.[91] They may also make an order where the application is made by a local authority, national park authority or statutory undertaker.

6.6.3 Orders made by the local planning authority under section 257 of the Town and Country Planning Act 1990

Although any highway may be diverted or extinguished by the Secretary of State under section 247, orders in respect of footpaths, bridleways or restricted byways[92] may also be made by local planning authorities under section 257. Indeed, in the Rights of Way Circular 1/09, 'Guidance for

---

87 For a case on procedure, see *Beckley Parish Council v Secretary of State for Transport* [2010] EWHC 606 (Admin).

88 TCPA 1990, s 253 as amended by Growth and Infrastructure Act 2013, s 11.

89 *Ashby v Secretary of State for the Environment* [1980] 1 WLR 673. See also *Sage v Secretary of State for the Environment, Transport and the Regions* [2003] UKHL 22 on what amounts to 'substantially completed'.

90 Under TCPA 1990, s 77.

91 TCPA 1990, s 78.

92 Restricted Byways (Application and Consequential Amendment of Provisions) Regulations 2006 (SI 2006/1177).

Local Authorities', Defra encourages local planning authorities to make the order:[93]

> The Secretary of State can make an order under section 247 of the 1990 Act where planning permission has been granted, or for example, where an application for planning permission is before him, either on appeal, or following call-in, and it is considered expedient to invoke the concurrent procedures under section 253 of the Act. Otherwise, he will expect to exercise his power only in exceptional circumstances, for example in relation to development of strategic or national importance.

Before authorising the stopping up or diversion of a footpath, bridleway or restricted byway, the competent authority must be satisfied that it is necessary to enable the development to be carried out. In England, an application for planning permission must have been made.[94] In Wales, planning permission must have been granted unless the development is permitted under a general or special development order, or is to be undertaken by a government department.

The competent authority or the Secretary of State may not confirm an order unless planning permission has been granted and it is necessary to authorise the stopping up or diversion in order for the development to be carried out in accordance with the permission.

Orders are made by the planning authority which granted the permission. No other authority has to be consulted.[95]

6.6.4 The tests

Both the Secretary of State and the planning authority have a discretionary power to stop up or divert paths. They are not under a duty to do so. There are no statutory guidelines as to how they should exercise their discretion.[96] But case law has made it clear that there is no power to reconsider the merits of the planning permission. Also, the Secretary of State has to take into account the effect the order would have on those entitled to the rights which would be extinguished if the order was made.

---

93 Defra, Rights of Way Circular 1/09, 'Guidance for Local Authorities' (Defra, 2009) para 10.1.

94 TCPA 1990, s 257, amended by Growth and Infrastructure Act 2013, s 12.

95 Procedure is governed by TCPA 1990, Sch 14 and the Town and Country Planning (Public Path Orders) Regulations 1993 (SI 1993/10).

96 See *K C Holdings (Rhyll) Ltd v Secretary of State for Wales and Colwyn Bay BC* [1990] JPL 353; *Vasiliou v Secretary of State* [1991] 2 All ER 77.

6.6.5 The moral

Developers should ascertain what rights of way cross the site at the earliest opportunity. Solutions to the problems they could cause should be sought before a planning application is submitted, otherwise the development may be delayed, or thwarted completely.

6.6.6 Orders extinguishing or diverting public rights of way crossing or entering proposed highway under section 248 of the Town and Country Planning Act 1990

The Secretary of State may make an order stopping up or diverting a highway which crosses or enters the route of a proposed or improved highway. The Secretary of State must be satisfied that it is expedient to make the order in the interests of the safety of users of the proposed highway or to facilitate the movement of traffic.

This section can be used where sections 14 and 18 of the HA 1980 are not available, as the highway is not a special or classified road.

6.6.7 Orders extinguishing vehicular use under section 249 of the Town and Country Planning Act 1990

The local planning authority may apply to the Secretary of State to convert a carriageway to a footpath or bridleway to improve the amenity of the area. Certain classes of vehicle or vehicles belonging to specified persons may be permitted to continue to use the route.

6.6.8 Orders extinguishing public rights of way over land held for planning purposes under sections 251 and 258 of the Town and Country Planning Act 1990

The Secretary of State, for all highways, and the planning authority, for footpaths, bridleways or restricted byways,[97] may extinguish public rights of way over land which has been acquired or appropriated by a local authority for planning purposes.

---

97 Restricted Byways (Application and Consequential Amendment of Provisions) Regulations 2006 (SI 2006/1177).

The Secretary of State or planning authority must be satisfied that there is or will be an alternative right of way or that one is not required.

6.7 Rail crossing orders

6.7.1 Tests for making the order

In order to improve public safety, the Transport and Works Act 1992 introduced into the HA 1980[98] new powers for closing and diverting footpaths, bridleways and restricted byways[99] over railway crossings.

Before making the order, the council must be satisfied that it is expedient to do so in the interests of the safety of members of the public who use, or are likely to use, the crossing.[100] Care must be taken to avoid the creation of a cul-de-sac route which would encourage trespass on the railway.[101]

A rail crossing diversion order must not alter the point of the termination of a path unless that point is on a highway over which there is at least a similar right of way or, where the point of termination is on such a highway, to another point on the same highway or one connected with it.

A stopping-up order may stop up the public right of way over the rail crossing alone, or it may in addition stop up the route on one or both sides of the crossing until its junction with another highway.

When confirming the order, the authority or the Secretary of State must be satisfied that it is expedient to do so in all the circumstances and, in particular, whether it is reasonably practicable to make the crossing safe and, if the order is to be confirmed, what arrangements have been made for barriers and signs to be erected and maintained.

The Secretary of State has power to require the operator to provide a tunnel or bridge, or to improve an existing tunnel or bridge to take the path under or over the railway instead of making the order.[102]

---

98 HA 1980, ss 118A and 119A.

99 Restricted Byways (Application and Consequential Amendment of Provisions) Regulations 2006 (SI 2006/1177).

100 HA 1980, s 118A(1).

101 Defra, Rights of Way Circular 1/09, 'Guidance for Local Authorities' (Defra, 2009) para 5.48.

102 Transport and Works Act 1992, s 48(2).

6.7.2 Procedure

An application for a stopping-up or diversion order must be made by the railway operator in the form prescribed by regulations.[103] The railway operator is the company responsible for maintaining the track. If a separate company operates the trains, it has no right to apply. The applicant must provide information on the need for the order and other alternative measures such as safety improvements to the crossing.

The Secretary of State has special reserve powers. If the authority has not made and confirmed an order, or submitted an opposed order for confirmation within 6 months of receiving a valid application, he may intervene and make an order himself without consulting the council.[104]

The HSE has produced guidelines on the safety requirements for footpaths and bridleways at level crossings.

6.8 Temporary diversions and closures

6.8.1 Engineering works

Statutes allow for temporary diversions for specific purposes. These include diversions of footpaths, bridleways and restricted byways for up to 3 months in connection with any excavation or engineering operation that is reasonably necessary for agricultural purposes. The highway authority will make an order, but it does not have to be advertised, nor is there any opportunity for objections to be made. A notice and plan must be displayed at either end of the diversion whilst it is in force.[105]

6.8.2 Animal disease and plant health

Defra may prohibit entry to a notified area infected by certain animal diseases, such as foot and mouth disease, or plant diseases such as

---

103 Rail Crossing Extinguishment and Diversion Orders Regulations 1993 (SI 1993/9), as amended by Rail Crossing Extinguishment and Diversion Orders, the Public Path Orders and the Definitive Maps and Statements (Amendment) Regulations 1995 (SI 1995/451) (the 'SI 1995/451 Regulations').

104 HA 1980, s 120(3A).

105 HA 1980, s 135, as amended by the Rights of Way Act 1990 and the Restricted Byways (Application and Consequential Amendment of Provisions) Regulations 2006 (SI 2006/1177).

rhizomania.[106] Public rights of way in the notified area may not be used. Contravention of any orders made by Defra will be an offence carrying a fine.

106 Animal Health Act 1981, s 23; Foot and Mouth Disease Order 1983 (SI 1983/1950), as amended by the Foot and Mouth Disease (Amendment) (England) (No 7) Order 2001 (SI 2001/1862); Plant Health (England) Order 2005 (SI 2005/2530).

7 Highway Authority

7.1 Duties of highway authority

The highway authority[1] has many duties and powers relating to public rights of way. These include making of improvement plans and public path orders, maintaining publicly maintainable rights of way including unblocking drains and felling trees,[2] and asserting and protecting the rights of the public to the use and enjoyment of rights of way.

The highway authority must:

- keep the surface of public rights of way which are maintained at public expense in a fit state for public use
- make sure obstructions are removed
- maintain some bridges over natural watercourses, including farm ditches
- provide at least a 25% contribution to landowners' costs for replacing and maintaining structures for the control of animals, e.g. gates or stiles, on completion of the work to a standard the highway authority is satisfied with
- make sure there are no notices that prevent or discourage the use of a public right of way
- add signs where a public right of way leaves metalled roads
- make sure the public's rights to use a public right of way are protected
- make sure landowners carry out their duties, and take action if they don't.[3]

Anyone can report an obstruction to the local authority and request that it be removed. The authority must respond to all requests within 1 month to confirm receipt, contact the person who complained to tell them what action is being taken and ensure the obstruction is removed, either by the local authority or the person responsible for it.

---

1 For definition, see HA 1980, s 1.

2 *Vernon Knight Associates v Cornwall Council* [2013] EWCA Civ 950; *R (Dillner) v Sheffield City Council* [2016] EWHC 945 (Admin).

3 Natural England Guidance, 'Public rights of way: local highway responsibilities', available at www.gov.uk/guidance/public-rights-of-way-local-authority-responsibilities.

If the obstruction is not removed within 2 months of receipt of the complaint, the person who complained can apply for a court order to have it removed. The magistrates' court may then take out an order against the local highway authority for the removal of the obstruction.

7.2 Legal interest of highway authority

7.2.1 Public maintainable highways

Where a highway is publicly maintainable, the surface is vested in the highway authority. Section 263(1) of the HA 1980[4] provides, '... every highway maintainable at the public expense, together with the materials and scrapings thereof, vests in the highway authority who are for the time being the highway authority for the highway'.

The question of whether a highway is maintainable at public expense is complex. But as a guiding principle, public rights of way will be publicly maintainable if they are created formally or if they were created before 16 December 1949.[5]

7.2.2 The extent of the public maintainable highway

The highway authority has a statutory form of determinable fee simple in that its interest lasts until the highway is stopped up or diverted. However, that interest does not extend up to the sky and down to the centre of the earth. The interest in the airspace and below the surface is limited to that which is required by the authority for the exercise of its powers and the performance of its statutory duties. In the words of Lord Herschell in *Tunbridge Wells Corpn v Baird*,[6] 'The interest of the highway authority is that which is necessary for its control, protection and maintenance as a highway for public use'.

There is no statutory definition of the extent required. Lord Denning, in *Tithe Redemption Comrs v Runcorn Urban District Council*,[7] referred to 'the top spit, or perhaps, I should say the top two spits of the road ...'.

The question most often arises in connection with the laying of pipes, wires, cables and other apparatus in the highway. It has also arisen in relation to possession proceedings. In *Wiltshire County Council v Frazer*,[8] it

---

4 This provision was first introduced by Public Health Act 1848, s 68.

5 See 7.3.1.

6 [1896] AC 434.

7 [1954] 2 WLR 518.

8 (1984) 47 P&CR 69.

was held that the highway authority's ownership of the surface enabled it to bring an action for possession against squatters who had set up their caravans on the highway.

The width of the highway is also an important issue. Where rights of way are entered on the definitive map, the width may be specified in the statement accompanying the map. If not, the width may be ascertained from other documents. Failing that, the width will be the historic use of the route.[9]

There are also presumptions in relation to highways which may be relevant, depending on whether there is: (1) a metalled road; (2) fences or dykes; (3) ditches; or (4) no defined track:

(1) The public are not confined to using only the metalled road. It may be that the verges of the road have also been dedicated to the public use. But where a metalled road crosses unenclosed land, and there is no indication of the limits of the highway by fences, ditches, etc., then the presumption is that the public right of way is limited to the metal track.[10]

(2) If it is established that fences adjoining a highway were put up in order to separate it from the adjoining land, there is a presumption that the public are entitled to a right of passage over the whole space between the hedges and dykes unless there is evidence to the contrary.[11] However, there is no presumption that the fences were put up to separate the adjoining land from the highway.[12]

    The fence may have nothing to do with the highway.[13] For instance, the fence may be so far away from the road that it cannot have any connection with it; or the fence may have been put up for the purpose of separating farmland from waste.

(3) Ditches, such as those normally made by owners on the boundaries of their property, are not presumed to be part of the highway.[14] However, it is possible for ditches to be piped and filled in and

---

9 *Easton v Richmond Highway Board* (1871) LR 7 QB 69.

10 *Belmore (Countess) v Kent County Council* [1901] 1 Ch 873.

11 *Sinclair v Kearsley* [2010] EWCA Civ 112.

12 *Hale v Norfolk County Council* [2001] 2 WLR 1481, qualifying *Attorney General v Beynon* [1970] 1 Ch 1.

13 *Hinds and Diplock v Breconshire County Council* [1938] 4 All ER 24.

14 *Hanscombe v Bedfordshire County Council* [1938] 1 Ch 944.

dedicated as part of the highway. Moreover, ditches are sometimes made specifically for draining the highway.[15]

(4) Where there is a public right of passage over a field or open space but no defined track, then the right is probably confined to a strip of reasonable width running between specified points.

Sometimes highways are created as a result of statute or by orders or agreements. These may, and sometimes must, specify the widths.[16]

7.2.3 Non-publicly maintainable highways

If a highway is not publicly maintainable, the surface as well as the subsoil will remain vested in the landowner. However, the highway authority has powers of control over the highway and could therefore be liable in nuisance for obstruction.

7.3 Maintaining of public rights of way

7.3.1 Public rights of way which are publicly maintainable

Dedication before 16 December 1949

At common law, the general rule was that the inhabitants of a parish were liable to repair all highways within the parish. The Highways Act 1835[17] provided that in order for highways dedicated after the Act came into force to be publicly maintainable, a procedure had to be followed. The Act did not apply to footpaths or bridleways which continued to be repairable by the public at large.

Section 47 of the National Parks and Access to the Countryside Act 1949 (NPACA 1949) declared that all existing public paths were repairable by

---

15 *Chorley Corpn v Nightingale* [1907] 2 KB 637.

16 Town and Country Planning (Public Path Orders) Regulations 1993 (SI 1993/10), amended by the SI 1995/451 Regulations; Public Path Orders Regulations 1993 (SI 1993/11), amended by the SI 1995/451 Regulations; Wildlife and Countryside (Definitive Maps and Statements) Regulations 1993 (SI 1993/12), amended by (SI 1995/451 Regulations); Rail Crossing Extinguishment and Diversion Orders Regulations 1993 (SI 1993/9), amended by the SI 1995/451 Regulations. See also the Planning Inspectorate, Rights of Way Section, Advice Note No 16, 'Widths on orders' (May 2003), available at www.gov.uk/government/publications/rights-of-way-advice-note-16-widths-on-orders.

17 Highways Act 1835, s 23.

the inhabitants at large. Therefore, it was considered that the duty to maintain such paths would lie with the parish, even if there had been no formal adoption. Section 49 of the NPACA 1949 expressly provided that section 23 of the Highways Act 1835 should apply to all paths dedicated after the commencement of the 1949 Act. In other words, such paths would no longer be publicly maintainable unless one of the provisions discussed below applied.

Paths created by public path creation orders or agreements

Section 38 of the Highways Act 1959 provided that footpaths and bridleways created after the passing of the Act, pursuant to public path creation orders and agreements, should be maintained at public expense.

Formally adopted paths

A landowner may expressly dedicate a public right of way, but unless it is formally adopted following the statutory procedures, it will not be maintainable at public expense. To do this, he must give notice of the proposed dedication to the highway authority and repair it for at least 12 months.[18]

Diverted paths

Paths diverted pursuant to diversion orders, including special and Site of Special Scientific Interest (SSSI) diversion orders, and agreements will be maintainable at public expense.[19] Informal diversions, on the other hand, will not be publicly maintainable.

Roads used as public paths, restricted byways and byways open to all traffic

RUPPs, reclassified under the WLCA 1981 as footpaths, bridleways or BOATs, are publicly maintainable.[20]

If a RUPP was reclassified under the CA 1968, the path become publicly maintainable 'as from the date of publication of the definitive map and statement in the special review'.[21] Therefore, if the map was published,

---

[18] HA 1980, s 37.

[19] HA 1980, s 36(2)(d)–(f); Restricted Byways (Application and Consequential Amendment of Provisions) Regulations 2006 (SI 2006/1177).

[20] WLCA 1981, s 54(4); CROWA 2000, s 47.

[21] CA 1968, Sch 3, para 9(2)(a).

the path would become publicly maintainable. The position is preserved by the CROWA 2000.

Where a RUPP was shown on a draft map and statement on a review under NPACA 1949 and was then shown on the definitive map and statement as a BOAT, bridleway or footpath under the provisions of section 55 of the WLCA 1981, the reclassified path is publicly maintainable.[22]

Many of the special reviews were abandoned in accordance with section 55 of the WLCA 1981. If it can be proved that the reclassification was to have been to a footpath or bridleway and that the path existed in December 1949, then the paths are publicly maintainable under that Act.

Restricted byways came into existence on 2 May 2006, the date of the commencement of sections 47 and 48 of the CROWA 2000, and from that date became highways maintainable at public expense.[23] Any other liability to maintain under a special enactment or by reason of tenure, enclosure or prescription was extinguished.

If a BOAT was added to the definitive map by a modification order[24] rather than a reclassification order, maintenance liability depended on when the BOAT was shown to have been created. If it was created before 1835, then it will be publicly maintainable. If after that date, it will have had to have been formally adopted.

It may be that the BOAT was created under statute or an inclosure award which sets out who is responsible for maintenance.

Deemed dedication

Where a public right of way comes into existence on the basis of user which occurs after 1949, there will be no one responsible for maintenance unless the path is formally adopted by the highway authority. If the path had legal existence before 16 December 1949, it will be publicly maintainable.

7.3.2 List of streets

Every highway authority must make and keep up to date a list of streets within its area which are highways maintainable at public expense.[25] The

---

22 WLCA 1981, s 55, as amended by CROWA 2000, Sch 5, Pt I, para 5.

23 CROWA 2000, s 49.

24 National Environment and Rural Communities Act 2006, s 67 prevents, subject to limited exceptions, further BOATs being added to the definitive map.

25 HA 1980, s 36(6).

list may be kept electronically.[26] 'Street' is defined to include[27] '... any highway and any road, lane, footpath, square, court, alley or passage, whether a thoroughfare or not, and includes any part of a street'.

The list may be inspected at the county council's offices free of charge. The county council is obliged to supply each district within the county with an up-to-date list of publicly maintainable streets within the area of the district. This, too, may be inspected free of charge at the relevant district office.[28]

7.3.3 Meaning of 'maintenance'

'Maintenance' is defined to include repair.[29] Maintenance, or a duty to repair, does not include the removal of obstructions. The leading case is *Hereford and Worcester County Council v Newman*,[30] in which there were several problems relating to three footpaths. A distinction was made between want of repair and obstruction. A hawthorn fence and other vegetation growing on the surface of the path made the paths out of repair, but wire fences and overhanging vegetation did not; they were obstructions.

A highway is not out of repair when blocked by natural and man-made obstructions. However, maintenance is not limited to repair, and the removal of silt, debris and vegetation could come within the duty to maintain.[31]

There is no duty on a highway authority to improve rather than maintain a highway.

7.3.4 Ordinary traffic

Where a highway authority is liable for maintenance, it must keep the highway in such a state as to be safe and fit for the ordinary traffic of the neighbourhood at all seasons of the year.[32] Where the ordinary traffic increases over time, the duty of repair is increased. The converse, however, is not true.

---

26 *Fortune v Wiltshire County Council* [2012] EWCA Civ 334: strict compliance with s 36 was not required.

27 HA 1980, s 329.

28 HA 1980, s 36(7).

29 HA 1980, s 329.

30 [1975] 1 WLR 901.

31 *Department for Transport, Environment and the Regions v Mott Macdonald* [2006] EWCA Civ 1089.

32 *R v High Halden (Inhabitants)* (1859) 1 F&F 678.

Where liability is imposed on, say, a railway undertaking or a canal company, whether the standard of repair will increase depends on the particular Act under which the railway or a canal was constructed. There have been several cases where there was no obligation on the canal company to strengthen a bridge to carry the heavier vehicles which were currently using the bridge.[33]

Where a BOAT has been added to the definitive map by a modification order, or a RUPP has been reclassified as a BOAT, there is no obligation on a highway authority to provide a metalled carriageway or a carriageway which is by any other means provided with a surface suitable for the passage of vehicles.[34] Nor is there any obligation for a highway authority to provide on a restricted byway a metalled carriageway or carriageway which is by other means provided with a surface suitable for cycles or other vehicles.[35]

Although a bicycle may be ridden on a bridleway, the highway authority is under no obligation to do anything to facilitate the use of the bridleway by cyclists.[36]

As to what is the required standard for the maintenance of footpaths or bridleways, there are no statutory guidelines. It depends on the amount of use, where the path is situated and by whom it is likely to be used. The surface of the path must not create a hazard, but, as Cumming-Bruce LJ said in *Littler v Liverpool Corporation*,[37] 'A highway is not to be criticised by the standards of a bowling green'.

7.3.5 Extraordinary traffic

If a publicly maintainable highway is damaged by traffic of excessive weight or by other extraordinary traffic, the highway authority may recover the extra expense incurred from the person causing the damage.[38] Proceedings have to be started within 12 months of the damage occurring or, where there is a contract for work extending over a period of time, within 6 months of the completion of that contract. However, before a claim may be made or expenses recovered, there must be a certificate from the highway authority's proper officer to the effect that extraordinary

---

33 E.g. *Sharpness New Docks and Gloucester & Birmingham Navigation Co v Attorney-General* [1915] AC 654.

34 WLCA 1981, s 54(7) (now repealed).

35 CROWA 2000, s 49(4).

36 CA 1968, s 30(3).

37 [1968] 2 All ER 343.

38 HA 1980, s 59.

expenses have been or will be incurred by the authority in maintaining the highway.

It may be difficult to ascertain what amounts to extraordinary traffic. In *Hill v Thomas*, Bowen LJ gave some guidelines. He stated:[39]

> ... extraordinary traffic is really a carriage of articles over the road, at either one or more times, which is so exceptional in the quality or quantity or articles carried, or in the mode or time of user of the road, as substantially to alter and increase the burden imposed by ordinary traffic on the road and to cause damage and expenses thereby beyond what is common.

A claim for extraordinary traffic is most likely to be made in the public rights of way context where four-wheel drive vehicles use BOATs in unsuitable conditions so that they destroy the surface of the road. However, it is difficult to see how this can be extraordinary traffic, as BOATs carry rights for mechanically propelled vehicles.

7.3.6 Public and private rights

The duty of the highway authority is to maintain a public right of way for the ordinary traffic. If there is, therefore, a public bridleway or footpath, the authority is not under a duty to repair it for the use of vehicles by the landowner or other person with a private right.

However, the landowner or person entitled to the benefit of a private right of way has no right to interfere with the surface of the right of way which is vested in the authority. He would therefore need the authority's consent and possibly planning permission. The simpler course would be to persuade the authority to do the work in return for payment of the additional costs.

Even if the public right of way is not publicly maintainable, the person with the private vehicular right may have problems in upgrading the surface of the route. He may find that in order to do so, he will be committing a number of criminal offences, as it is likely to involve the obstruction of the route. He could, therefore, be guilty of public nuisance or of committing offences under the HA 1980 (e.g. removing soil or turf from any part of a highway,[40] wilfully). However, where a private right of way pre-dates the dedication of the public right, the dedication will be subject to rights already granted. A private right of way under an express grant carries an implied ancillary right to maintain and improve. (A

---

39 [1893] 2 QB 333, 340–341.

40 HA 1980, s 131.

prescriptive right entitles the grantee to maintain only. There is no right to improve.[41])

Planning permission will not be necessary if the works do not extend beyond the boundaries of the existing route. The carrying out of works required for the maintenance or improvement of the street or way on land within the boundaries of an unadopted street or private way is permitted development within the Town and Country Planning (General Permitted Development) Order 1995.[42]

7.3.7 Erosion

A practical problem often arises where a riverside or cliff path is eroded. If the path is maintainable at public expense, the question is whether the highway authority is under an obligation to maintain the path or whether it can allege that the path has been extinguished by its physical disappearance.

The answer to these questions will depend to a large extent on the factual situation. However, it is suggested that where a cliff path has disappeared, it will usually be impractical for the path to be repaired and, indeed, the right of way will cease to exist along with the maintenance liability.

The same is true where there is a riverbank path that is eroded.[43] However, this is likely to be a more gradual process, and the highway authority is probably under a duty to shore up the path before it disappears. In deciding whether the highway has been destroyed, it seems that the court may have regard to whether it would be economic to do the repairs.[44]

7.3.8 Enforcement of duty to repair

The duty to repair is enforced by following the procedures set out in section 56 of the HA 1980:

(1) A notice must be served on the highway authority or other person who it is considered is liable to repair the highway. A notice requires the recipient to state whether he admits that the way or bridge is a highway and that he is liable to repair it.

---

41 *Mills v Silver* [1991] Ch 271.

42 (SI 1995/418), art 3, Sch 2, Pt 9.

43 *R v Secretary of State for the Environment, Transport and the Regions ex parte Gloucestershire County Council* [2000] EGCS 150.

44 *R v Greenhow Inhabitants* (1876) 1 QBD 703.

(2) Within 1 month of receiving such a notice, the recipient must state whether he agrees that the highway is maintainable by him or, if the recipient is a highway authority, that it is repairable at public expense.

(3) When the complainant has received the notice of admission, he has 6 months to apply to a magistrates' court for an order requiring the highway to be repaired. The magistrate will decide whether the highway is out of repair. If it is out of repair, the court will stipulate a time within which the repairs should be done.

(4) If the highway has not been put into repair at the end of that period, the magistrate may extend the period or authorise the complainant to do the work. The complainant can then recover the expenses of so doing as a civil debt from the highway authority or other person against whom the order was made.

If no notice of admission is given within 1 month of the original notice, the complainant may apply to the Crown Court to determine whether the highway is a highway and whether the respondent is liable to repair it.

If either the magistrates' court or the Crown Court orders the person responsible for maintenance to carry out the work by the end of a specified period and this is not done, the complainant may apply to the magistrates' court for an order authorising him to carry out the works himself.

The magistrates' court may either extend the period for doing the works or make a new order authorising the complainant to do the work. If he does the work, he can recover expenses as a civil debt.

7.3.9 Liability for failure to maintain

Section 41 of the HA 1980 imposes on a highway authority a duty to maintain highways which are maintainable at the public expense.

In order to make out a claim for damages under section 41, it is necessary to show that the highway is dangerous to traffic, i.e. likely to cause physical injury or damage. It does not enable an adjoining landowner to claim economic loss because his business suffers due to the want of repair of the road.[45]

In ascertaining whether a highway is dangerous to traffic, foreseeability is an important element. The danger must have been caused by the breach of the duty to maintain the highway.

---

45 *Wentworth v Wiltshire County Council* [1993] 2 WLR 175.

The House of Lords held in *Goodes v East Sussex County Council*[46] that a highway authority's duty under section 41(1) of the HA 1980 is an absolute duty to maintain the fabric of the highway in such good repair as to render the physical condition safe for ordinary traffic to pass at all seasons of the year. However, the duty to maintain did not include a duty to prevent the formation of ice or remove the accumulation of snow on the road.[47] As a result of this case, section 41A was added to the HA 1980.[48] Local authorities now have to ensure as far as is reasonably practicable that the safe passage along a highway is not endangered by snow and ice.

The duty to maintain does not extend to traffic signs and road markings,[49] nor is there liability under section 41 for the layout of the highway.[50]

7.3.10 The statutory defence

A highway authority has a defence to an action against it in respect of its failure to maintain a highway maintainable at the public expense.[51] A highway authority must show that it has taken such care as in all the circumstances is reasonably required to secure that the part of the highway to which the action relates is not dangerous for traffic.

The court is directed to take into account:

(1) the character of the highway, and the traffic which was reasonably to be expected to use it;

(2) the standard of maintenance appropriate for a highway of that character and used by such traffic;

(3) the state of repair in which a reasonable person would have expected to find the highway;

(4) whether the highway authority knew, or could reasonably have been expected to know, that the condition of the part of the highway to

---

46 [2000] 1 WLR 1356. See consequential amendments made to Road Traffic Act 1988, s 21(2)(b) and HA 1980, s 300 introduced by CROWA 2000, s 70.

47 In *Sandhar v Department of Transport, Environment and the Regions* [2004] EWCA Civ 1440, it was held that there was no common law duty of care to salt the roads and so there was no liability in negligence.

48 Section inserted by Railways and Transport Act 2003, s 111.

49 *Gorringe v Calderdale Metropolitan Borough Council* [2004] UKHL 15, [2004] 1 WLR 1057.

50 *Thompson v Hampshire County Council* [2004] EWCA Civ 1016.

51 HA 1980, s 58.

which the action relates was likely to cause danger to users of the highway;[52] and

(5) where the highway authority could not reasonably have been expected to repair that part of the highway before the cause of action arose, what warning notice of its condition had been displayed.

However, for the purposes of such a defence, it is not relevant to prove that the highway authority had arranged for a competent person to carry out or supervise the maintenance of the part of the highway to which the action relates, unless it is also proved that the authority had given him proper instructions with regard to the maintenance of the highway and that he had carried out the instructions.

Most of the cases concerned with the statutory defence relate to urban pavements. However, a case in which the council was successful in relation to a footpath was *Whiting v Hillingdon Borough Council*.[53] The plaintiff stepped into some undergrowth at the side of the path to allow someone to pass. She injured her leg on a tree stump which was obscured by vegetation. The path had been regularly inspected and had been repaired 2 months before the accident. The court held that the council had exercised reasonable care and was not obliged to beat the foliage for hidden traps or dangers.

Councils should therefore ensure that they have a regular inspection regime in force and that they keep records of such inspections. They should be able to show that they have cleared the actual surface of the path and have repaired any serious defects such as potholes. Drainage and other remedial actions may be called for in specific situations, or notices warning of hazards.

7.3.11 Extinguishment of liability

Liability to maintain will cease when the highway is extinguished or the maintenance liability is extinguished by court order.

A highway authority may apply to the magistrates' court to extinguish the maintenance liability on the ground that the highway is not needed for public use.[54] However, an application may not be made in respect of footpaths or bridleways.

---

52 Regular inspections are obviously important. See *Pridham v Hemel Hempstead Corpn* (1970) 69 LGR 523.

53 (1970) 68 LGR 437. See also *Owen v City of Westminster* [2004] EWHC 1577 (Admin).

54 HA 1980, s 47(1).

If after an order has been made there is a change of circumstances, an application may be made to the magistrates' court to remake the highway publicly maintainable.[55]

Extinguishment of the highway itself may occur where it physically ceases to exist (e.g. due to coastal erosion) or where there has been a successful application for extinguishment to the magistrates' court under section 116 of the HA 1980. Restricted byways, bridleways and footpaths may be extinguished under section 118 if the order is confirmed by the local authority or Secretary of State.

An individual's liability to repair may be extinguished by an agreement with the local authority. On the date specified in the agreement, the highway becomes maintainable at public expense.[56]

An individual's liability may also be extinguished by order of the magistrates' court or where there is a diversion under section 116.[57]

In both cases, the route or diverted route will become maintainable at public expense, if it is not so already, and the individual will have to pay compensation for being relieved of the responsibility.

7.4 Improvements plans[58]

7.4.1 Initial plan

Every local highway authority, other than an inner London authority (i.e. Transport for London, the council of an inner London borough or the Common Council of the City of London[59]), was required to prepare and publish a rights of way improvement plan within 5 years of the commencement of section 60 of the CROWA 2000.[60] Those authorities

---

55 HA 1980, s 48.

56 HA 1980, s 38.

57 HA 1980, s 54.

58 See Defra Guidance, 'Local authority rights of way improvement plans', available at www.gov.uk/guidance/local-authority-rights-of-way-improvement-plans.

59 CROWA 2000, s 60(5).

60 CROWA 2000, s 60(1).

which were categorised as excellent were relieved of their duty to prepare, publish or implement improvement plans.[61]

The local highway authority could make arrangements for its functions to be carried out jointly with any relevant district council or National Park authority.[62]

The plan had to contain the authority's assessment of:

(1) the extent to which the local rights of way met the present and likely future needs of the public;

(2) the opportunities which local rights of way provided for exercise and other forms of open-air recreation and enjoyment of the authority's area;

(3) the accessibility of local rights of way for the blind or partially sighted and others with mobility problems; and

(4) such other matters relating to local rights of way as the Secretary of State or the National Assembly might direct.

The plan had also to contain a statement of action which the authority proposed to take for the management of local rights of way and for seeking an improved local network, taking into account the matters dealt with in the assessment.

The Secretary of State and the Welsh ministers have power to require other material to be included in the improvement plan. They may also give guidance from time to time on the preparation and publication of improvement plans to which the highway authorities must pay due regard in carrying out their functions.

Local rights of way are defined as footpaths, cycle tracks (other than those at the side of or in a made-up carriageway), bridleways and restricted byways within the authority's area (whether shown on the definitive map or not) and ways within the authority's area which are shown on the definitive map as BOATs.

---

61 Local Authorities (Categorisation) (England) Order 2004 (SI 2004/1704); Local Authorities Plans and Strategies (Disapplication) (England) Order 2005 (SI 2005/157), art 6 disapplies the duties under s 60 of the CROWA 2000 to prepare and publish rights of way improvement plans, and makes further supplemental provision for cases where authorities have already prepared such plans, or have prepared and published, but not implemented, them.

62 CROWA 2000, s 61(5).

7.4.2 Reviews

An authority must make, within 10 years of the publication of the initial plan and subsequently at intervals of not more than 10 years, a new assessment of the local needs, review the plan and decide whether to amend it. If it decides to amend the plan, it must publish it in its amended form. If it decides not to amend it, it must publish a report of its decisions with reasons.[63]

7.5 Public path orders

7.5.1 General principles

Public path orders under the HA 1980 consist of creation orders,[64] stopping-up orders and diversion orders.[65] The procedures for making and confirming the orders are specified in regulations.[66] Powers of entry are given to survey the land in connection with orders and claims for compensation.[67]

7.5.2 Initiation of the process

The authority[68] may make an order on its own initiative, or a request for an order may be made by local residents, path users, farmers, landowners and anyone else.

---

63 CROWA 2000, s 60(3).

64 See Chapter 3. HA 1980, s 26.

65 See Chapter 6. HA 1980, ss 26, 118 and 119; TCPA 1990, ss 257, 258 and 261.

66 For orders made under HA 1980, ss 26, 118 and 119: Public Path Orders Regulations 1993 (SI 1993/11), amended by the SI 1995/451 Regulations; for orders made under HA 1980, ss 118A and 119A: Rail Crossing Extinguishment and Diversion Orders Regulations 1993 (SI 1993/9), amended by the SI 1995/451 Regulations; for orders made under HA 1980, s 118B or s 119B: Highways, Crime Prevention etc. (Special Extinguishment and Special Diversion Orders) Regulations 2003 (SI 2003/1479); for orders made under HA 1980, s 119D (diversion of certain highways for protection of SSSIs): Highways (SSSI Diversion Orders) (England) Regulations 2007 (SI 2007/1494), Sch 3.

67 HA 1980, s 293, as amended by CROWA 2000, Sch 6, Pt I, para 17.

68 The authority, for this purpose, is a county council, unitary authority, district council, London borough council, the Common Council of the City of London, Council of Welsh county or county borough, National Park Authority: HA 1980, s 329(1); Local Government Act 1992, ss 17–23; Local Government (Wales) Act 1994; Environment Act 1995.

It is important, where an application or a request is made, for the person who wants the order to have spoken to all those who might be affected by it. For instance, a farmer who wants a path closed or diverted should speak to the parish council and local user groups. Unless they are consulted and approve of the proposals, they are likely to object to the order. Preliminary discussions should also be held with the highway authority's rights of way officer.

7.5.3 Costs

Applicants may be liable to pay the costs of making an order.[69] Regulations[70] provide that the costs which local authorities may recover must not exceed the costs actually incurred.

Local authorities may waive all or part of the costs. They are likely to do so if the order benefits the public, as where an extra path is created. The fact that an order is not confirmed does not give the applicant an automatic right to a refund. Costs must be refunded, however, where the authority decides not to proceed with an order or the order is invalid.

Local authorities are encouraged to publish details of their policy on charging. Examples are given in Defra's Rights of Way Circular 1/09, 'Guidance for Local Authorities', of the costs that authorities may incur in making the order.[71]

The authority can require the applicant to enter into an agreement to pay, or contribute towards the costs of making up the new path and any compensation that may be payable, before it will make a diversion order.

7.5.4 Consultation

Before making an order, the authority has to consult any other local authority for the area (including the National Parks Planning Board, if there is one). There is no obligation to consult parish councils, the landowner or user groups. However, the authority is encouraged to do so. The Lake District and Peak District National Parks and the Norfolk and Suffolk Broads Authority have power to make applications. The authority must consult county and district councils.

---

69 Under HA 1980 ss 26, 118, 118A, 119 and 119A, but not for SSSI diversions under s 119D.

70 Local Authorities (Charges for Overseas Assistance and Public Path Orders) Regulations 1996 (SI 1996/1978).

71 Defra, Rights of Way Circular 1/09, 'Guidance for Local Authorities' (Defra, 2009) paras 5.34–5.36.

7.5.5 Deciding whether to make the order

The authority must be sure that the tests set out in the relevant Act for making the order are fulfilled. Even where they are, the authority has a discretion. It may decide not to make the order. There is no appeal against the authority's decision not to make an order, but the applicant can ask the Secretary of State to make the order. He will only do so in exceptional circumstances. The decisions about whether to make public path orders are made either by elected councillors, being members of a committee or panel or by officers to whom authority has been delegated by the order-making authority. Members of the public are not entitled to speak at meetings, but some authorities have adopted procedures which enable interested parties to make statements to committees.

Members of the public are entitled to attend meetings unless confidential or exempt information would be disclosed to them.[72]

Notice of meetings must be given at least 5 days before the meeting or, if the meeting is convened at shorter notice, at the time that it is convened.[73] In practice, many councils have annual timetables of meetings and dates are fixed some time ahead.

The agenda and papers for the meeting must be available at and before the meeting unless they relate to items during which the meeting is not likely to be open to the public.[74]

The minutes, a summary of the proceedings, agenda and reports must be available for inspection for 6 years after the date of the meeting.[75]

Background papers to the reports must also be available for inspection for 6 years after the date of the meeting.[76]

Authorities must maintain a register of council members with their names and addresses. They must also maintain a register of powers delegated to council officers.[77]

---

72 Local Government Act 1972, s 100(k).

73 Local Government Act 1972, s 100A(6); Local Authorities (Access to Meetings and Documents) (Period of Notice) (England) Order 2002 (SI 2002/715).

74 Local Government Act 1972, s 100B.

75 Local Government Act 1972, s 100C.

76 Local Government Act 1972, s 100C.

77 Local Government Act 1972, s 100G.

7.5.6 The order

The form of the order is set out in regulations.[78] The order should contain a plan to a scale of not less than 1:2,500 or to the scale of the largest published map for the area. It must be accompanied by a notice which:

(1) briefly describes the effect of the order;

(2) states where the order may be inspected free of charge and where a copy can be purchased;

(3) gives the address to which objections can be sent; and

(4) gives the date by which any objections must be made.

This must be at least 28 days after the notice of the order is first published.

7.5.7 Giving notice of a path order

The notice must be published in England on the authority's website or on such other websites or through the use of such other digital communications media as the authority consider appropriate. Where an order is made in Wales, the order must be published in a local newspaper.[79]

Notice of the order must be sent to anyone who has formally requested and paid for notice of such an order, and must be prominently displayed at council offices in the locality and at any other places the authority considers appropriate, such as on local parish notice boards.

In addition, the notice and plan must be displayed at the ends of the path affected by the order. The plan must show the effect of the order on the path.

The notice, plan and order must be sent to:

(1) any other local authorities in the area, including the parish council or meeting; and

(2) the owners, occupiers and lessees of any land affected by the order and the bodies prescribed in the regulations.

These bodies are, for all orders in England, the British Horse Society, the Byways and Bridleways Trust, the Cyclists Touring Club, the Open Spaces Society and the Ramblers' Association; in addition, where the path is in the relevant area, the Chiltern Society or the Peak and Northern Footpath Society.

---

78 See fn 66.

79 This is the existing position in Wales and also in England. HA 1980, Sch 6, para 1(3)(3ZA). Inserted by DA 2015, Sch 7, Pt 4, para 8(2) (not yet in force).

The Auto Cycle Union and the British Driving Society are prescribed bodies to receive copies of notices and orders, except those affecting footpaths and bridleways over which no public vehicular rights are claimed or suspected to exist.

7.5.8 Objections

Objections should be made in writing before the date set out in the notice. Objections may be made on the grounds that the tests set out in the Act have not been satisfied, that there are reasons why a path should not be created, diverted or extinguished or that the details of the order are unacceptable.

The DA 2015 has amended Schedule 6 to the HA 1980. When the relevant amendments are in force, the position will be as stated in the following paragraphs.[80]

The order-making authority may decide not to submit an order to the Secretary of State for confirmation if it considers that the representations or objections are not relevant to the decision of whether to confirm the order. The authority may confirm the order as if it were unopposed.

If one or more of the objections are relevant, the authority may make two orders: one comprising the parts to which the relevant objections relate, and the other, comprising the remaining parts, which is treated as if no objections had been duly made.

In making these decisions the authority must have regard to any guidance given by the Secretary of State and must inform the applicant and any person who made representations or objections of its decision and the reasons for it.[81]

The above provisions relating to irrelevant objections and representations apply in England, but not in Wales.

7.5.9 Unopposed orders

If there are no objections or the objections are withdrawn to the order, it can be confirmed by the local authority.[82] It should determine whether to do so or whether to submit the order to the Secretary of State as soon as reasonably practicable after the time for making representations has expired. Notice of the decision, with reasons, should be given to the

---

80 DA 2015, Sch 7, Pt 4, para 8(3) inserts para 2(2ZA)–(2ZE) into HA 1980, Sch 6 (not yet in force).

81 HA 1980, Sch 6, para 2(2ZD)–(2ZE) (not yet in force).

82 HA 1980, Sch 6, para 2(1).

applicant and any prescribed persons as soon as practicable after the decision has been made.[83] Where a determination has not been made within 2 months, beginning with the expiry of the time for making representations, the Secretary of State may, at the request of the person on whose application the order was made, direct the authority to determine the question before the time specified in the direction.[84]

Should the authority want to change the order, it must start the process again and make a new order or submit the order to the Secretary of State (even where there are no objections). He has power to confirm the order with modifications.

7.5.10 Opposed orders

If there are objections to the order, the authority may decide by formal resolution not to proceed with the order.[85] Subject to the points made in 7.5.8 about irrelevant objections, the usual procedure is to refer the order to the Secretary of State for confirmation. The authority should determine whether to submit the order to the Secretary of State as soon as reasonably practicable after the time for making representations has expired. Notice of the decision, with reasons, should be given to the applicant and any prescribed persons as soon as practicable after the decision has been made.[86]

As with unopposed orders where a determination has not been made within 2 months, beginning with the expiry of the time for making representations, the Secretary of State may, at the request of the person on whose application the order was made, direct the authority to determine the question before the time specified in the direction.[87]

Where the order is submitted to the Secretary of State, the authority may, in the light of objections received, ask the Secretary of State to modify the order. The Secretary of State may appoint an inspector to hold a public inquiry or hearing or deal with the matter by written representations.[88] These procedures are discussed in Chapter 9. However, he can decide not

---

83 HA 1980, Sch 6, para 2ZA(1) and (2) (not yet in force). Inserted by CROWA 2000, Sch 6, Pt I, para 23(6).

84 HA 1980, Sch 6, para 2ZA(3) (not yet in force). Inserted by CROWA 2000, Sch 6, Pt I, para 23(6).

85 *R (Hargrave) v Stroud District Council* [2002] EWCA Civ 1281.

86 HA 1980, Sch 6, para 2ZA(1) and (2) (not yet in force). Inserted by CROWA 2000, Sch 6, Pt I, para 23(6).

87 HA 1980, Sch 6, para 2ZA(3) (not yet in force). Inserted by CROWA 2000, Sch 6, Pt I, para 23(6).

88 HA 1980, s 302; Local Government Act 1972, s 250.

to do so if he considers that nothing in the representations or objections would be relevant in deciding whether to confirm the order.[89]

Where representations and objections made to an authority in England relate to only parts of the order, the Secretary of State may make two separate orders: one comprising the parts to which the objections or representations relate, the other comprising the remaining parts. The Secretary of State will then determine the opposed order and leave the other order for the authority to confirm.[90]

The inspector may confirm the order, refuse to confirm it or confirm the order with modifications. If the modifications are not of a minor nature, but, say, affect land not within the original order, the modified order must be re-advertised. If objections are received, a second inquiry may be necessary.

Modifications cannot be made to correct serious legal errors or discrepancies. A new order will have to be made regardless of the merits of the defective order.

7.5.11 Notice of confirmation

Notice of a confirmed order must be given by the authority in the same way as it gave notice of the making of the order.

If the order is not confirmed, the persons and organisations who were given notice of the making of the order must be informed. The authority does not have to publish the decision in the press or put up notices on the path.

7.5.12 Statutory review

The decision to confirm an order made by the inspector may be challenged only where he has exceeded his powers or where the proper procedures have not been followed. This provision has been interpreted to include mistakes of law.

An application to the High Court must be made within 42 days of the decision. The court may quash *the decision* of the Secretary of State confirming the order or any part of it instead of quashing *the order* or any

---

89 WLCA 1981, Sch 13A, para 8(2) (not yet in force). Inserted by DA 2015, Sch 7, Pt 2, para 6.

90 HA 1980, Sch 6, para 2ZZA (not yet in force). Inserted by DA 2015, Sch 7, Pt 4, para 8(6).

provision of it.[91] The order may not be challenged in any other legal proceedings whatsoever.[92]

7.5.13 Judicial review

Where an inspector decides not to confirm the order, the decision may be challenged on the grounds of illegality, irrationality or procedural impropriety,[93] amongst other things. An application for leave for judicial review should be made without delay and, in any event, within 3 months of the decision.

7.5.14 Effect of the confirmed order

The order may specify when it will come into operation. This may be when the order is confirmed, at a stated time after the confirmation of the order or when certain works have been completed. This applies particularly in development cases. Because of the delay that can arise, a further notice of the coming into operation of the order has to be published to inform the public of the change. If the development is not carried out or the new path is not certified as completed, an order, although confirmed, may never come into operation.

The definitive map and statement is amended after the path order is brought into operation. The amendment is made by a legal events modification order.[94] Because the order merely records what has already taken place, it does not have to be advertised, nor is there any scope for objections.

Ordnance Survey has to be notified of the confirmed order and the date it comes into operation. The alteration will be made to the Ordnance Survey map on the next revision.

Even though it is purely an administrative procedure, there can sometimes be a delay of several years after the public path order is in operation before the legal event order is made. There is a new power, introduced by the CROWA 2000,[95] whereby joint public path and definitive map orders may be made, thus cutting down delay and bureaucracy.

---

91 HA 1980, Sch 6, para 3A(2) (not yet in force). Inserted by DA 2015, Sch 7, Pt 4, para 8(8).

92 HA 1980, Sch 2, para 4. See also WLCA 1981, Sch 15, para 12.

93 *Council of Civil Service Unions v Minister for the Civil Service* [1984] 3 All ER 935, 949–951.

94 WLCA 1981, s 53(2) and (3)(a)(i) and (ii).

95 CROWA 2000, Sch 5, Pt I, para 2, inserting s 53A into the WLCA 1981. Public Rights of Way (Combined Orders) (England) Regulations 2008 (SI 2008/442). See Defra, 'Combined Orders and the power to include modifications in other orders: Guidance for surveying authorities to accompany SI 2008/442' (Defra, 2008).

It is the responsibility of the authority for the area to see that any new path created by order is properly signposted and waymarked. There is no legal obligation to put up notices stating that paths have been closed by orders, although sometimes it would be helpful to do so.

7.6 Crime prevention

7.6.1 Special extinguishment orders for crime prevention and school security[96]

Local highway authorities may make orders stopping up certain highways for purposes of preventing or reducing crime, which would otherwise disrupt the life of the community, in areas designated by the Secretary of State.[97] The powers extend to footpaths, bridleways, restricted byways (whether on the definitive map or not) and such paths if shown on the definitive map but over which the public have a right of way for vehicular and all other kinds of traffic. The highway authority may also stop up highways shown on the definitive map as BOATs, but there is no power to stop up a trunk or special road.

Before the power can be exercised, it must be shown that premises adjoining or adjacent to the highway are affected by high levels of crime and the existence of the highway is enabling persistent commission of criminal offences.

An order will not be confirmed unless the Secretary of State, or the highway authority for uncontested orders, is satisfied that those conditions have been fulfilled and that it is expedient to confirm the order. In particular, regard must be paid to any strategy for the reduction of crime and disorder prepared under section 6 of the Crime and Disorder Act 1998, any alternative routes and the possibility of a diversion rather than a stopping-up order and the effect that the extinguishment will have on other land served by the highway, taking into account the compensation provisions.[98] Where an order is contested, it is for an inspector to decide

---

96 CROWA 2000, Sch 6, Pt I, para 8; HA 1980, s 118B.

97 Crime Prevention (Designated Areas) Order 2004 (SI 2004/1239); Crime Prevention (Designated Areas) Amendment Order 2004 (SI 2004/2674); Crime Prevention (Designated Areas) Order 2005 (SI 2005/829); Crime Prevention (Designated Areas) (No 2) Order 2005 (SI 2005/914); Crime Prevention (Designated Areas) (No 3) Order 2005 (SI 2005/2463); Crime Prevention (Designated Areas) Order 2006 (SI 2006/302); Crime Prevention (Designated Areas) Order 2007 (SI 2007/1829). See also Defra, 'Guidance for local authorities: on crime prevention on public rights of way-designation of areas' (February 2003).

98 See HA 1980, ss 118B, 119B, 121(2) and 28.

whether the benefits of closure outweigh any adverse effects the closure would have on the public.[99]

The highway authority may also stop up the highways specified above which cross land occupied for the purposes of a school, in order to protect pupils and staff from:

(1) violence;

(3) alarm or distress arising from unlawful activity; or

(4) any other risk to their health or safety arising from such activity.

Provision was made under the HA 1980[100] for the proprietor of the school to make an application to the highway authority for a special extinguishment order. These provisions, like those enabling landowners of agricultural land to make applications, have not been brought into force.[101]

A school security extinguishment order will not be confirmed unless it is expedient to do so, having regard to any other security measures which could have been taken, whether the order will achieve a substantial improvement in that security, the availability of an alternative route, the possibility of a diversion rather than a stopping-up order and the effect that the closure will have on any other land served by the highway, taking into account provisions for compensation.

It is important to stress that the making and confirmation of an order is a two-stage process with different tests. In *R (Hockerill College) v Hertfordshire County Council*,[102] the school applied for a special extinguishment order. This was refused by the council. The school then applied for judicial review of the decision, which was quashed on the grounds that the council had confused the separate tests, applying the requirements which applied at the confirmation stage rather than those at the order-making stage.

Before making a special extinguishment order, either for crime prevention or school security, the council must consult the police authority for the area in which the highway lies.

The form of special extinguishment orders and the scale of the map which is required has been prescribed by regulations.[103] Schedule 6 to the

---

99 *R (Manchester City Council) v Secretary of State for the Environment, Food and Rural affairs* [2007] EWHC 3167 (Admin).

100 HA 1980, s 118C.

101 See 6.4.3

102 [2008] EWHC 2060 (Admin).

103 Highways, Crime Prevention etc. (Special Extinguishment and Special Diversion Orders) Regulations 2003 (SI 2003/1479); Highways (Schools) Special Extinguishment and Special Diversion Orders (Wales) Regulations 2005 (SI 2005/1809).

HA 1980 governs the making, confirmation, validity and date of operation of the orders.

7.6.2 Gating orders and public space protection orders

Local authorities could make gating orders on grounds of crime and anti-social behaviour.[104] These enabled public access to be restricted on highways, including public rights of way, but they did not remove highway status from the routes. In *Ramblers Association v Coventry City Council*,[105] the court held that there was sufficient evidence of criminal offences or anti-social behaviour facilitated by the existence of the footpath to justify the making of an order. The local authority had not erred in exercising its powers to make the gating orders. Under section 129A(3)(c) of the HA 1980, the test to be applied was whether it was 'expedient to make a gating order', and it was not proper to import into that test a requirement of reasonable necessity. What was expedient depended on all the circumstances. Relevant considerations for a local authority to have regard to when considering whether to impose a blanket restriction included available resources and the utility, cost and practicality of a lesser restriction.

Gating orders have been replaced by public space protection orders made under Chapter 2 of Part 4 of the Anti-Social Behaviour, Crime and Policing Act 2014. The public space protection orders are intended to deal with existing or potential nuisances in a particular area by imposing conditions on the use of that area. Before making an order, the authority must publicise the proposed order and consult the chief officer of police, the Police and Crime Commissioner (or the equivalent in London) and any representatives of the local community it considers appropriate. Orders will last for up to 3 years before requiring a review.[106] However, there is no limit on the number of times an order can be reviewed and renewed. The two-part test for issuing the order will be that the authority is satisfied on reasonable grounds that that activities carried on, or likely to be carried on, in a public place are detrimental to the local community's quality of life, and that the impact justifies restrictions being

---

[104] Clean Neighbourhoods and Environment Act 2005, s 2, inserting new ss 129A–129G into HA 1980. The regulations were: Highways Act 1980 (Gating Orders) (England) Regulations 2006 (SI 2006/537) and Highways Act 1980 (Gating Orders) (Wales) Regulations 2007 (SI 2007/306).

[105] [2008] EWHC 796 (Admin).

[106] Anti-Social Behaviour, Crime and Policing Act 2014, s 60(1).

put in place in a particular area. The behaviour must also be ongoing and unreasonable.[107]

Where an order restricts access to a public right of way, the local authority should also consider the impact on occupiers of premises adjoining or adjacent to the route, and on others in the locality. Where the right of way is a through route, the authority should also consider the availability of a reasonably convenient alternative.[108]

The Act provides that:

> (4) A public spaces protection order may not restrict the public right of way over a highway for the occupiers of premises adjoining or adjacent to the highway.
>
> (5) A public spaces protection order may not restrict the public right of way over a highway that is the only or principal means of access to a dwelling.
>
> (6) In relation to a highway that is the only or principal means of access to premises used for business or recreational purposes, a public spaces protection order may not restrict the public right of way over the highway during periods when the premises are normally used for those purposes.

The local authority must inform those in the locality of any proposed order.[109] Where an order would restrict a public right of way that crosses into another local authority area, that local authority must also be consulted where the issuing authority thinks it appropriate to do so.[110]

7.6.3 Guidance for local authorities

Defra's Rights of Way Circular 1/09, 'Guidance for Local Authorities', contains useful information with links to relevant statutory instruments.[111]

---

107 Anti-Social Behaviour, Crime and Policing Act 2014, s 59(2)(3).

108 Anti-Social Behaviour, Crime and Policing Act 2014, s 64(1).

109 Anti-Social Behaviour, Crime and Policing Act 2014, s 64(2).

110 Anti-Social Behaviour, Crime and Policing Act 2014, s 64(3).

111 See www.gov.uk/government/uploads/system/uploads/attachment_data/file/69304/pb13553-rowcircular1-09-091103.pdf.

8 Surveying Authority

8.1 Introduction

The councils which are the highway authorities are also the surveying authorities. These are the 'council of the county, metropolitan district or London borough'. In Wales, the county or county borough is the surveying authority.[1]

The surveying authorities have duties and powers. Duties impose an obligation on the councils; powers give them a discretion. Both the duties and powers relate to the definitive map, i.e. the map which records rights of way. The purpose is to make sure that public rights of way are properly identified and do not disappear through non-use. The system for registering public rights of way was introduced by the NPACA 1949. The surveying authorities were under a duty to prepare a definitive map and statement covering the rights of way in their area. They have a continuing duty to keep it up to date.

The DA 2015, which at the time of writing has not been brought into effect, has made several changes which impact on the surveying authorities' duties. Part 3 of the WLCA 1981 has been amended so as to:

(a) alter the test that applies where a local authority is deciding whether to modify a definitive map and statement on the basis of evidence relating to the existence of a right of way not currently shown on the map;

(b) enable regulations to be made to simplify the procedure that applies where a modification of a definitive map and statement is needed because of an administrative error;

(c) enable regulations to be made so that applications made to a local authority seeking a modification of a definitive map and statement do not need to be included in the register of applications unless the authority have given notice that there is a reasonable basis for the applicant's belief that the map should be modified;

---

1 HA 1980, s 31(7).

(d) facilitate the making of modifications of a definitive map and statement by consent in cases based on documentary evidence of the existence of a right of way before 1949.[2]

In short, the DA 2015 has introduced in England new streamlined and simplified procedures for updating the definitive map where applications are made for modification orders. These, it is hoped, will result in better quality applications and a reduction in conflict and disputes. In England, Schedules 14 and 15 to the WLCA 1981 will be replaced by new Schedules 13A and 14A. Schedules 14 and 15 continue to apply in Wales.[3]

8.2 The duties

8.2.1 To keep the map and statement under continuous review

The surveying authority is under a duty to keep the map up to date, taking into account events which occurred before the coming into event of the WLCA 1981 as well as subsequently.[4]

Alterations to the map are made by means of modification orders. There are powers for the surveying authority to prepare an updated version of the map or maps[5] incorporating the modification orders.

A surveying authority may make modifications orders of its own accord, and is under a duty to do so where there has been a legal event order under section 53(3)(a) of the WLCA 1981.

Any person may apply for a modification order under section 53(3)(b) and (c) of the WLCA 1981. The application has to be made on a form prescribed by regulations[6] and must be accompanied by evidence in support. The evidence may be a combination of documentary evidence and user statements. The map must be on a scale of 1:25,000. This provision was satisfied in a case[7] where the map had been digitally enlarged from an original map which was on a scale of 1:50,000.

---

2 DA 2015, s 26.

3 DA 2015, Sch 7, Pt 2, para 6, Sch 13A, Pt 3, para 7, Sch 14A (not yet in force).

4 WLCA 1981, s 53(2)(a).

5 WLCA 1981, ss 57 and 57A.

6 WLCA 1981, Sch 14. Wildlife and Countryside (Definitive Maps and Statements) Regulations 1993 (SI 1993/12).

7 *R (Trail Finders Fellowship) v Dorset County Council* [2013] EWCA Civ 553.

The authority must keep a register of applications for modification orders.[8] However, under the DA 2015,[9] the Secretary of State may, by regulations, provide that the duty does not apply unless the applications have passed the new preliminary assessment procedure and notice has been given to every owner and occupier of the land to which the application relates.

8.2.2 To comply with the new preliminary assessment procedure (provisions not in force at time of writing)

Parts 2 and 3 of Schedule 7 to the DA 2015 have introduced a new Schedule 13A in England replacing Schedule 14 which still applies in Wales. There is no preliminary assessment procedure in Wales.

An applicant for a modification order must be made on a prescribed form with a map drawn to prescribed scale, and must include copies of any documentary evidence in support of the application, unless the authority have informed the applicant that the authority already have access to a particular document. Each application must contain an explanation as to why the applicant believes that the definitive map and statement should be modified.[10]

A surveying authority must, within three months of receiving an application for a modification order, decide whether there is a reasonable basis for the applicant's belief that the definitive map should be altered on the statutory grounds set out in the WLCA 1981.[11] These are:

> the expiration, in relation to any way in the area to which the map relates, of any period such that the enjoyment by the public of the way during that period raises a presumption that the way has been dedicated as a public path or restricted byway;
>
> ... or the discovery by the authority of evidence which (when considered with all other relevant evidence available to them) shows—
>
> (i) that a right of way which is not shown in the map and statement subsists[12] over land in the area to which the map relates, being a right of way such that the land over which the right subsists is a public path,

---

8 WLCA 1981, s 53(3)(c).

9 WLCA 1981, s 53B(4)(a) and (b) (not yet in force).

10 WLCA 1981, Sch 13A, para 1(1) and (2) (not yet in force) inserted by DA 2015, Sch 7, Pt 2, para 6.

11 WLCA 1981, s 53, Sch 13A, para 2(1) (not yet in force).

12 The words 'reasonably alleged to subsist' have been deleted by DA 2015, Sch 7, Pt 1, para 2 (not yet in force), but retained for Wales.

a restricted byway or, subject to section 54A, a byway open to all traffic;

(ii) that a highway shown in the map and statement as a highway of a particular description ought to be there shown as a highway of a different description; or

(iii) that there is no public right of way over land shown in the map and statement as a highway of any description, or any other particulars contained in the map and statement require modification.

In making such a decision, the surveying authority must have regard to any guidance given by the Secretary of State.[13]

If the authority decides there is no basis for the decision, it must inform the applicant giving its reasons.[14] If, on the other hand, the authority decides there is a reasonable basis, it must inform the applicant and serve notice on every affected landowner and occupier, stating that it is investigating an application that has been made.[15]

Where it is not possible to ascertain the owner or occupier, the authority may put the notices on the land concerned.[16]

Failure of an authority to carry out a preliminary assessment within 3 months of receiving an application gives the applicant a right to apply to the magistrates' court. The applicant must give 1 month's notice of his intention to apply to the court and must then do so within 6 months.[17]

The court has power to order the authority to take specified steps for discharging its duty and to do so within a specified time. The authority or the applicant can appeal to the Crown Court against any decision. An order of the magistrates' court will not take effect until 21 days after it has been made or, if there is an appeal, until it is determined or withdrawn.[18]

8.2.3 To determine the application

The surveying authority must, as soon as reasonably practical after serving notice on affected landowners and occupiers, investigate the matters stated in the application, consult the relevant authorities and decide whether to make the order.[19] Notice of the decision with reasons for it

---

13 WLCA 1981, Sch 13A, para 2(2) (not yet in force).

14 WLCA 1981, Sch 13A, para 2(4) (not yet in force).

15 WLCA 1981, Sch 13A, para 2(3) (not yet in force).

16 WLCA 1981, Sch 13A, para 2(5) (not yet in force).

17 WLCA 1981, Sch 13A, para 3(1)(2) (not yet in force).

18 WLCA 1981, Sch 13A, para 3(3)(5)(6) (not yet in force).

19 WLCA 1981, Sch 13A, para 4(1) (not yet in force).

must be given to the applicant and also to the landowners and occupiers notified after the preliminary assessment.[20]

However, where a modification order is made by consent under section 54B of the WLCA 1981, the duty to serve notice on landowners and occupiers and consult the relevant authorities does not apply[21] unless:[22]

(a) the authority ascertains that the owner does not consent to the making of an order;

(b) the authority decides for any other reason not to make the order;

(c) 12 months, from the date when notice was served on affected landowners and occupiers, stating that an application had been made and the authority were considering it,[23] expire without the authority deciding whether to make the order;

(d) the authority makes the order but decides not to confirm it.

8.3 Result of determination

8.3.1 Failure to make a decision

Where an authority fails to make a decision within 12 months of receiving an application, the applicant and any affected landowners or occupiers can apply to the magistrates' court. This does not apply where the application has been dismissed under the preliminary assessment procedure.

Notice of intention to apply to the court must be given to the surveying authority on the prescribed form.[24] The applicant must supply the court with the names and addresses of any other persons who could have served a notice, unless he informs the court that it is not practical to do so.[25] Notice of the hearing, the right to be heard and the right to appeal

---

20 WLCA 1981, Sch 13A, para 4(4) (not yet in force).

21 WLCA 1981, Sch 13A, para 4(2) (not yet in force).

22 WLCA 1981, Sch 13A, para 4(3) (not yet in force).

23 WLCA 1981, Sch 13A, para 2(4)(b) (not yet in force).

24 WLCA 1981, Sch 13A, para 5(1) (not yet in force).

25 WLCA 1981, Sch 13A, para 6(1)(2) (not yet in force).

must be given to such persons.[26] The court must also put the information on some conspicuous object on the affected land.[27]

The application to the magistrates' court must be made after 1 month but not later than 12 months after such notice.[28] On the hearing of the application, the other persons by whom a notice could have been given have a right to be heard.[29] The court may order the authority to take specified steps within a reasonable time in relation to the application for modification of the definitive map.[30] The authority may make one application to the magistrates' court to extend the time specified in the order for a period not exceeding 12 months.[31] The applicant for the order and the affected landowners and occupiers who could have given a notice of an intention to apply to the court have a right to be heard.[32] The requirements as to notice apply to the application for an extension as they do to the original hearing.[33] There is a right of appeal to the Crown Court.[34]

Any order of the magistrates' court will not take effect until 21 days after it has been made or an appeal is determined by the Crown Court or, by way of case stated, by the High Court.[35]

8.3.2 Decision not to make an order

Where a surveying authority decides not to make a modification order, the applicant can, within 28 days after the service of notice of the decision, give notice of his wish to appeal and the grounds for doing so to the authority.[36] Regulations will prescribe the form of the notice. The authority must submit the matter to the Secretary of State for a decision, and the Secretary of State must deal with it as an appeal against the authority's decision.[37] The authority must give notice that it has done so.

---

26 WLCA 1981, Sch 13A, para 6(4) (not yet in force).

27 WLCA 1981, Sch 13A, para 6(5) (not yet in force).

28 WLCA 1981, Sch 13A, para 5(2) (not yet in force).

29 WLCA 1981, Sch 13A, para 5(3) (not yet in force).

30 WLCA 1981, Sch 13A, para 5(4) (not yet in force).

31 WLCA 1981, Sch 13A, para 5(5) (not yet in force).

32 WLCA 1981, Sch 13A, para 5(6) (not yet in force).

33 WLCA 1981, Sch 13A, para 6(4) and (5) (not yet in force).

34 WLCA 1981, Sch 13A, para 5(7) (not yet in force).

35 WLCA 1981, Sch 13A, para 5(8) (not yet in force).

36 WLCA 1981, Sch 13A, para 7(1) (not yet in force).

37 WLCA 1981, Sch 13A, para 7(2) (not yet in force).

The surveying authority can decide not to submit the appeal to the Secretary of State if it considers that the grounds of appeal are irrelevant.[38] The authority must have regard to any guidance given by the Secretary of State[39] and must inform the applicant of its reasons for not submitting the appeal.[40]

Where the matter is submitted to the Secretary of State, the authority must give notice:

(a) setting out the authority's decision;

(b) stating that the matter has been submitted to the Secretary of State;

(c) naming a place in the area in which the land to which the decision relates is situated where a copy of the decision may be inspected free of charge, and copies of it may be obtained at a reasonable charge, at all reasonable hours; and

(d) specifying the time (not being less than 42 days from the date of the first publication of the notice) within which, and the manner in which, representations or objections with respect to the decision, which must include particulars of the grounds relied on, may be made to the Secretary of State.[41]

There are provisions about the publication of the notice on the website, and the service of notice on owners and occupiers, other relevant local authorities and interested persons.[42] Copies of the notices must be displayed on the path and in the local council offices and other places specified in regulations.

The Secretary of State must decide the appeal through a public inquiry, a hearing or written representations, unless he considers that nothing in the grounds of appeal or in the representations or objections are relevant.[43]

The Secretary of State may decide that the order should not be made, or direct the authority to make an order or make the order himself.[44] There are detailed provisions for the holding of hearings, public inquiries and the appointment of inspectors.[45]

---

38 WLCA 1981, Sch 13A, para 7(3) (not yet in force).

39 WLCA 1981, Sch 13A, para 7(4) (not yet in force).

40 WLCA 1981, Sch 13A, para 7(5) (not yet in force).

41 WLCA 1981, Sch 13A, para 7(6) (not yet in force).

42 WLCA 1981, Sch 13A, paras 7(7), (8), (9), (10), (11) and (12) (not yet in force).

43 WLCA 1981, Sch 13A, para 8(1)(2) (not yet in force).

44 WLCA 1981, Sch 13A, para 8(3) (not yet in force).

45 WLCA 1981, Sch 13A, para 9 (not yet in force).

8.4 Modifications arising from administrative errors

The Secretary of State is given powers to provide for Schedules 13A and 14A to apply with prescribed modifications to the making of orders under section 53(2) where there have been administrative errors.[46] The surveying authority must be satisfied that:

(a) it is requisite to make a modification of a definitive map and statement in consequence of an event mentioned in section 53(3)(c) (i.e. there is evidence that a right of way, or a way with higher rights should be shown on the definitive map or that a public right of way should not have been shown or any of the particulars are incorrect);

(b) the need for the modification has arisen because of an administrative error; and

(c) both the error and the modification needed to correct it are obvious.

In deciding whether the conditions above apply, the authority must have regard to any guidance given by the Secretary of State.

8.5 Legal event orders

A modification order should be made to record that the status of the highway has been changed through the coming into operation of any enactment or instrument or any other event, both before and after the commencement date of the WLCA 1981. These events are divided into three.[47]

The first event is where the highway has been authorised to be stopped up, diverted, widened or extended.

A stopping-up or diversion order will usually be made under the HA 1980. There are powers under the same Act to widen a public path, but in order to effect such a widening, it may be necessary to get the agreement of the adjoining landowner or to have a compulsory purchase order or public path creation order. If the path were to be extended, then a creation agreement or order would be necessary.

The second category of legal events is where a highway of a particular description has ceased to be a highway of that description. This would

---

46 WLCA 1981, s 53ZA (not yet in force). Inserted by DA 2015, Sch 7, Pt 1, para 3.

47 WLCA 1981, s 53(3)(a)(i), (ii) and (iii).

cover greater rights over a footpath or bridleway created by agreement or order, or where the path has been downgraded as a result of an order.

The third category of rights is where the new right of way, being a public path (i.e. footpath or bridleway), has been created either by agreement or order.

Any order should include the addition to the statement of particulars of the position and width of any right of way which is or is to be shown on the definitive map and any limitations or conditions over it.[48]

Section 53A of the WLCA 1981 makes it possible for surveying authorities to include in legal event orders provisions to modify the definitive map and statement without the need for a separate modification order. Regulations have prescribed the orders covered by the section and the procedure to be followed.[49]

8.6 Consent orders

Where there is documentary evidence of the existence of a right of way before 1949, an authority may make a consent modification order if certain conditions are fulfilled.[50] Where there is an application under section 53(5) of the WLCA 1981, the authority must have served notice under paragraph 2(4)(b) of Schedule 13A that they are considering the application.[51] However, it is not necessary for an application to have been made if there is evidence that a right of way exists or that there is a period of use by the public which raises a presumption of deemed dedication.

Every owner of the land to which the application relates must consent to the making of the order. If they consent, the local authority can make the order which must contain a statement that it is made with the consent of every owner. However, landowners might consent only if certain changes are made to the alleged right of way. The local authority has power to make special orders, namely a diversion order or an order altering the width of the path or an order imposing a new limitation or condition on the use of the right of way, provided all the affected landowners consent.

---

48 WLCA 1981, s 53(4).

49 Public Rights of Way (Combined Orders) (England) Regulations 2008 (SI 2008/442). The orders covered are: HA 1980, ss 26, 118, 118(A), 118B(4), 119, 119A and 119B(4); Acquisition of Land Act 1981, s 32; Housing Act 1985, s 294; and TCPA 1990, ss 247(2A), 257 and 258(1).

50 WLCA 1981, s 54B (not yet in force). Inserted by DA 2015, Sch 7, Pt 1, para 5.

51 Under WLCA 1981, Sch 13A, para 2(4)(b) (not yet in force). Inserted by DA 2015, Sch 7, Pt 2, para 6.

The modification order must contain in a single document the consent statement and also the special order.

Before making a diversion order, the authority must be satisfied that the path or way will not be substantially less convenient to the public in consequence of the diversion and have regard to any guidance given by the Secretary of State. The path cannot be diverted onto land owned by another landowner without that landowner's consent. An authority may not make a diversion order so as to alter a point of termination of a path if that point is not on a highway or where it is on a highway otherwise than to another point which is on the same highway, or a highway connected with it, and which is substantially as convenient to the public.[52]

If work is needed to bring the path into a fit condition for public use, the order cannot be confirmed until the authority is satisfied that the work has been carried out.

An authority must decide whether to make an order before 12 months have elapsed since the authority first notified the landowner of its decision that the definitive map and statements should be modified. The Secretary of State may extend the period by order.[53]

8.7 Procedure where a modification order is made

This procedure applies to orders other than those made pursuant to a direction given by the Secretary of State to the local authority or orders made by the Secretary of State.[54]

Before making an order, the authority must consult with every local authority whose area includes the land to which the order relates.[55] The requirements for the publicity of the order are similar to those set out in the section above for notices of an appeal to the Secretary of State.[56]

An order made either by the authority or the Secretary of State must be confirmed before it can take effect.[57] The Secretary of State must confirm the

52 WLCA 1981, s 54(C) (not yet in force). Inserted by DA 2015, Sch 7, Pt 1, para 5.

53 WLCA 1981, s 54B(9) and (10) (not yet in force). Inserted by DA 2015, Sch 7, Pt 1, para 5.

54 WLCA 1981, Sch 14A, Pt 2, para 2 (not yet in force). Inserted by DA 2015, Sch 7, Pt 3, para 7.

55 WLCA 1981, Sch 14A, Pt 2, para 3 (not yet in force).

56 WLCA 1981, Sch 14A, Pt 2, para 5 (not yet in force).

57 WLCA 1981, Sch 14A, Pt 2, para 4 (not yet in force).

order where he has directed the authority to make the order.[58] The authority may confirm a modification consent order or an order to which there are no outstanding representations or objections.[59] If there are modifications to the order, they must be confirmed by the Secretary of State.[60]

The authority can decide not to submit the order to the Secretary of State where it considers that the representations or objections would not be relevant in deciding whether to confirm the order. The authority must have regard to any guidance from the Secretary of State and must inform the applicant and any person who made representations or objections of their decision and the reasons for it.

An authority may sever an opposed order so that the Secretary of State may consider the disputed section only.[61] There is also power not to submit those parts of the order where the authority considers that the objections or representations are irrelevant. The Secretary of State may also sever an order.[62]

The Secretary of State may make his decision by holding an inquiry or hearing or through written representations.[63] Hearings and public inquiries are governed by the provisions in section 250(2) to (5) of the Local Government Act 1972 and section 322A of the TCPA 1990.[64] If he decides to make significant changes to an order, the modified order must be publicised and any objections or representations taken into account.[65]

The decision may be made by a person appointed by the Secretary of State, or he may call in a decision to make it himself.[66]

Notice of the confirmed order and the date it took effect, together with information of where copies of the order may be inspected, must be publicised in the same way as the original order.[67] If an order is not confirmed, notice of the non-confirmation must also be given. A person may challenge a confirmed order by application to the High Court. The grounds for a challenge are that it is not within the powers of sections 53,

---

58 WLCA 1981, Sch 14A, Pt 1, para 1 (not yet in force).

59 WLCA 1981, Sch 14A, Pt 2, paras 9 and 10 (not yet in force).

60 WLCA 1981, Sch 14A, Pt 2, para 11 (not yet in force).

61 WLCA 1981, Sch 14A, Pt 2, para 6 (not yet in force).

62 WLCA 1981, Sch 14A, Pt 2, para 12 (not yet in force).

63 WLCA 1981, Sch 14A, Pt 2, para 13 (not yet in force).

64 WLCA 1981, Sch 14A, Pt 2, para 16 (not yet in force).

65 WLCA 1981, Sch 14A, Pt 2, para 14 (not yet in force).

66 WLCA 1981, Sch 14A, Pt 2, para 15 (not yet in force).

67 WLCA 1981, Sch 14A, Pt 2, para 17 (not yet in force).

54, 54B or 54C or that any of the requirements of Schedule 13A or Schedule 14A of the WLCA 1981 have not been complied with.[68]

The High Court may quash the order or parts of it or may quash the decision of the Secretary of State. The ability to quash the decision rather than the order is a new provision to prevent a fresh order having to be made.

8.8 Wales

In Wales, as already mentioned, Schedule 14 to the WLCA 1981 continues to apply even after Schedule 14A is in force in England. This means there is no preliminary assessment procedure, all documentary evidence supporting the application must be supplied even if the authority already has the information, and the applicant himself has to serve notice of the application on the landowner.

Where an authority does not decide an application within 12 months, representations may be made to the Secretary of State. After consulting with the authority, the Secretary of State may direct the authority to determine the application within a specified time limit.

Where the authority decides not to make an order, the applicant can appeal to the Secretary of State, not the magistrates' court as in England. If he decides that an order should be made he can give directions to the authority to make the order, but he cannot make the order himself.

Schedule 15 also continues to apply in Wales. There must be consultation with every local authority whose area includes land to which the order relates, orders must be confirmed either by the authority or the Secretary of State and publicity must be given to the orders. This must include publication of a definitive map order in at least one newspaper circulating in the area. There is no power for the surveying authority to decide not to submit the order to the Secretary of State where the objections are not relevant to the Secretary's decision to confirm the order.

There is a power to sever an opposed order so that the Secretary of State need only consider the disputed part. The authority can confirm unopposed orders. Opposed orders must be submitted to the Secretary of State for confirmation.

Where the Secretary of State proposes to make significant modifications to an order, the modified order must be published and objections and representations taken into account.

---

68 WLCA 1981, Sch 14A, Pt 3, para 18 (not yet in force).

A decision may be made by a person appointed by the Secretary of State, or he may make the decision himself. Hearings and public inquiries are governed by the provisions in section 250(2) to (5) of the Local Government Act 1972 and section 322A of the TCPA 1990.

There are provisions for publicity of the final decisions on orders. Orders may be quashed by the High Court if sections 53 and 54 or the requirements of Schedule 15 have not been complied with.

8.9 Cut-off date

Although the definitive map is conclusive evidence as to what is recorded, the converse is not true. There may be perfectly valid rights of way which are not recorded. Claims to such rights based on evidence which pre-dates 1949 may be difficult and time-consuming to determine. The CROWA 2000[69] provides that unrecorded rights of way created before 1949 will be extinguished, subject to exceptions, immediately after 1 January 2026. This is known as the cut-off date.

It is anticipated that just before that date, there will be a flurry of applications to add unrecorded routes to the definitive map. Interested parties such as user groups will be undertaking research to establish claims to these paths. As local authorities are under a duty to keep the definitive map under review, there is a concern that they may be duplicating the work done by the voluntary sector.

In order to deal with this problem, the DA 2015 has introduced a new section into the CROWA 2000[70] which gives the Secretary of State power to make regulations enabling a surveying authority to designate, for a period of one year from the cut-off date, public rights of way which have been extinguished. The effect of such designation is that those paths will be treated as if they had not been extinguished. During that time, the authority must decide whether to show the right of way on the definitive map and statement. If the authority decides to do so, the right of way will remain unextinguished. On the other hand, if the authority decides not to do so, the right of way will be extinguished again.

These provisions will mean that the surveying authorities can wait until after the cut-off date to do their research. They will know at that stage whether research has been done by individuals or voluntary organisations and can designate those paths where no research has been done. Thus

---

69 CROWA 2000, ss 53–56 and Sch 5.

70 CROWA 2000, s 56A (not yet in force). Inserted by DA 2015, s 21.

they can concentrate on researching the designated paths and avoid duplicating the work done by others.

8.10 Protection for recorded rights of way created before 1949

An authority may not after the cut-off date make a modification order removing a recorded footpath, bridleway, restricted byway or BOAT from the definitive map if the only basis for the application is evidence that the right of way did not exist before 1 January 1949.[71]

---

[71] CROWA 2000, s 55A (not yet in force). Inserted by DA 2015, s 20.

9 The Planning Inspectorate

9.1 Introduction

Once a local authority has made a public path order, or a definitive map order, to which objections are duly made, the order has to be referred to the Secretary of State for confirmation, modification or refusal of confirmation (unless, in the case of a public path order, the council decides to withdraw the order[1]). The Secretary of State may deal with the matters by written representations, public inquiry or a hearing. The Secretary of State or the Welsh ministers have discretion as to whether to hold a public inquiry or hearing into a definitive map modification order if the only objections are not relevant to the decision whether to confirm the order.[2]

If there are no objections to an order, the local authority may itself confirm the order. Where objections are received to a public path order, it may decide to withdraw the order by formal resolution.[3] However, once the order has been passed to the Secretary of State for confirmation, this option is no longer available unless all objections are withdrawn.

The Rights of Way (Hearing and Inquiry Procedure) (England) Rules 2007[4] apply to modification and public path orders in England submitted to the Secretary of State on or after 1 October 2007. The aim of the rules is to ensure that all the parties have as much information as possible before the start of the inquiry or hearing.

The Planning Inspectorate's publication[5] explains the rules and gives a timetable for the various steps which must be taken by the parties. Similar guidance is given where the matter is dealt with by written representations (which are not covered by the rules).

---

1 *R (Hargrave) v Stroud District Council* [2002] EWCA Civ 1281.

2 CROWA 2000, s 51, and Sch 5, para 11, inserting para 7(2A) into WLCA 1981, Sch 15.

3 *R (Hargrave) v Stroud District Council* [2002] EWCA Civ 1281.

4 (SI 2007/2008).

5 The Planning Inspectorate, 'Guidance on procedures for considering objections to definitive map and public path orders in England' (October 2018), available at www.gov.uk.

Set out below is a summary of the main rules which apply to inquiries and hearings.

Rule 4 relates to the initial stages of a hearing or inquiry and provides for notification in relation to the hearing or inquiry to be given by the Secretary of State to the authority which made the order, to any applicant for the order, to every person who has made (and not withdrawn) representations or objections to the order and to certain other persons required to be notified in consequence of the HA 1980, the WLCA 1981 or the TCPA 1990.

Part 3 (rules 5 to 14) sets out the procedure for hearings and includes provision for submission of statements of case (rule 6), appearances at the hearing (rule 8) and site inspections and adjourning the hearing to the land (rule 9).

Part 4 (rules 15 to 26) sets out the procedure for inquiries and includes provision for pre-inquiry meetings (rule 15), submission of statements of case for the inquiry (rule 17), appearances at the inquiry (rule 19), proofs of evidence (rule 20), adjournments (rule 21) and site inspections and adjourning the inquiry to the land (rule 22).

Part 5 (rule 27) sets out the procedures for hearings and inquiries where a rights of way order is modified.

Part 6 (rules 28 to 32) relates to general matters and includes provision for allowing further time for taking steps under the rules (rule 28), inspection and copying of documents (rule 29) and the use of electronic communications (rule 31).

9.2 Public path orders

The local authority has power to make public path orders under sections 26, 118, 118A, 118B, 119, 119A, 119B and 119D of the HA 1980 and sections 257, 258 and 261 of the TCPA 1990.

Where the order is referred to the Secretary of State because there are objections to the order, the Planning Inspectorate will check that the order complies with the relevant regulations.[6]

If the Planning Inspectorate considers that the order does not comply with the regulations, it will be returned to the authority. The authority may then make another order.

---

6 See Defra, Rights of Way Circular 1/09, 'Guidance for Local Authorities' (Defra, 2009) Ch 5.

Besides checking that the order complies with the regulations, the Planning Inspectorate will ensure that all the correct documents accompany the order. These include the statement of reasons why the authority considers the order should be confirmed, the objections and the authority's comments on the objections. The Planning Inspectorate has produced a checklist of documents which must accompany the order.[7]

The local authority should also confirm that it has complied with any requirements under the relevant Act for consulting other local authorities and statutory undertakers.

If an order has been made under the HA 1980, the authority must send the Inspectorate a certificate showing that the organisations specified under the regulations have been consulted.

Sometimes, the authority which makes the order will not be supporting it. In such situations, the authority must state who will be supporting the order.[8] The authority may take a neutral stance or appear at the inquiry or hearing as an objector.

9.3 Definitive map orders[9]

The surveying authority is under a duty, if the criteria set out in the WLCA 1981 are met, to make orders modifying the definitive map.[10]

If objections are made to the order, the order is sent to the Secretary of State for confirmation. The Planning Inspectorate will check that it conforms with the Wildlife and Countryside (Definitive Maps and Statements) Regulations 1993.[11]

If the Planning Inspectorate considers that the order does not comply with the regulations, it will be returned to the authority. The authority may then make another order.

---

7 The Planning Inspectorate, 'Rights of way: order making authority checklist' (updated May 2017), available at www.gov.uk.

8 See the Planning Inspectorate, Rights of way advice note 1, 'Conduct of inquiries into orders' (November 2018), available at www.gov.uk.

9 See the Planning Inspectorate, 'Definitive map orders: consistency guidelines', available at www.gov.uk/government/publications/definitive-map-orders-consistency-guidelines.

10 WLCA 1981, s 53.

11 (SI 1993/12).

As with public path orders, the Planning Inspectorate also checks that all the necessary documents, including statement of reasons, objections and the authority's comments on the objections, have been sent with the order.

Sometimes, the authority which makes the order will not be supporting it. In such situations, the authority must state who will be supporting the order.[12] This is likely to occur where an authority has refused to make an order and the applicant has made an appeal to the Secretary of State.[13] The authority may take a neutral stance or appear at the inquiry or hearing as an objector. It may also happen that, after the authority has made the order, more evidence is discovered which results in the authority considering that the order should not be confirmed.

9.4 The procedures

The Secretary of State will decide whether to confirm the order on the basis of written representations, public inquiry or a hearing. He will write to the authority, or supporters of the order, where the local authority is not supporting a modification order, and the objectors stating the procedure to be followed. Generally, he will appoint an inspector, selected from the Lord Chancellor's panel of independent inspectors, to act on his behalf.

Procedural irregularities in regard to applications to modify the definitive map under Schedule 14 to the WLCA 1981 are not a matter for the inspector.[14] Any challenge must be by way of judicial review of the authority's decision. The procedural requirements relating to the order-making stage under Schedule 14 or Schedule 15 are a matter for the inspector.[15] Where they cannot be remedied without prejudice to the parties, the order should not be confirmed.

The same principles apply to applications for public rights of way orders. Procedural defects at the application stage can only be challenged by judicial review. Procedural defects at the order-making stage should be corrected if possible; if not, the order cannot be confirmed.

---

12 See the Planning Inspectorate, Rights of way advice note 1, 'Conduct of inquiries into orders' (November 2018), available at www.gov.uk.

13 The Planning Inspectorate, Rights of way advice note 1, 'Conduct of inquiries into orders' (November 2018), paras 23, 24 and 25, available at www.gov.uk.

14 The exception is where the inspector is considering whether the transitional provisions under NERCA 2006, s 67 apply.

15 See the Planning Inspectorate, Rights of way advice note 21 'Procedural irregularities' (May 2013), available at www.gov.uk.

9.5 Written representations

This procedure may be followed where the orders have attracted only a few objections, with none from the county or district council. It is not suitable where there is complex or lengthy evidence. The local authority or objectors may insist that the matter should be heard by an inspector.

Where the Planning Inspectorate considers that the order is suitable for determination by written representations, it will write to the local authority, the applicant and any other relevant persons asking for their agreement to the procedure, including the rules for the exchange of evidence and comments which is set out in Annex B of the Planning Inspectorate's Guidance. These are not statutory rules.

The steps to be taken are as follows:

(1) The Planning Inspectorate gives notice to the local authority, the applicant, relevant persons, prescribed organisations and anyone else whom the local authority was required to inform when it made the order that the written representations procedure is to be followed.

(2) The local authority must send its statement of case and supporting documents to the Planning Inspectorate within 2 weeks of the date specified in the notice (the start date). The statement of case is then sent by the Planning Inspectorate to the relevant parties and anyone who has made a written representation with information where the documents can be examined.

(3) The recipients of the statement of case have 8 weeks from the start date in which to submit their own statement of case. The Planning Inspectorate copies these to all the parties, including the local authority.

(4) Any comments on all or any of the statements of case must be received by the Planning Inspectorate not later than 14 weeks after the start date.

If during the course of these exchanges it is considered that the written representation procedure is no longer appropriate or is not being correctly adhered to, the Planning Inspectorate can arrange for a hearing or public inquiry instead.

It has been held that, where there was an opposed public path order, a supporter of the order who had written to the council had made a representation and was entitled to be treated as a party to the written representation procedures. She should therefore have been supplied with copies of the documents and given an opportunity to comment on them.[16]

The next stage is for the inspector to make a site visit. Objectors can ask to accompany the inspector. If they do so, the local authority must also be present. If the inspector decides that an accompanied visit is necessary, the Planning Inspectorate will give at least 2 weeks' notice of the time and place it will take place.

The purpose of the site visit is for the inspector to see the order route and surrounding paths and to note the physical features. During the site visit, the inspector cannot discuss the arguments of either side.

If further evidence is sent to the inspector by an entirely new party after the deadlines but before he makes his decision, and it is material to the decision, he will send the evidence to everyone who has made written representations and give them the opportunity to reply. In extraordinary circumstances, late evidence may be accepted from a party who is already involved.

9.6 Hearing procedure

9.6.1 When will it be used?

The Planning Inspectorate has decided that in some cases it would be better to have a hearing rather than a public inquiry. This is because public inquiries may be too formal and intimidating for members of the public. Hearings are often used in planning appeals.

The procedure is not suitable if there are:

(1) too many people wanting to speak;

(2) complicated policy matters;

(3) important legal issues; or

(4) a need for cross-examination.

The procedure is governed by the Rights of Way (Hearings and Inquiries Procedure) (England) Rules 2007.[17]

---

16 *R v Secretary of State for the Environment ex parte Slot* [1998] JPL 692.

17 (SI 2007/2008).

9.6.2 What is a hearing?

A hearing is a discussion led by the inspector who will decide the case. Everyone involved will sit around a table, usually in a small committee room.[18]

The inspector will explain what the hearing is about. He will set out the issues as he understands them, having read the papers, visited the site and asked for clarification, if necessary, on points arising on the order or plans.

Everyone around the table may ask questions and discuss the issues.

There will then be a site visit. Some of the issues may be discussed at the site itself if all the parties are able to attend. Sometimes, however, the hearing will have closed before the site visit taking place. Where this happens there can be no further discussion.

9.6.3 Procedure relating to the hearing

The Planning Inspectorate gives notice in writing of the hearing to the local authority, other relevant local authorities, the applicant and landowners and occupiers, relevant persons, prescribed organisations and anyone else who has made known their interest in the order. The notice will give the start date, the time and place of the hearing, describe the land to which the order relates and the effect of the order. It must also specify where the documents can be inspected and the date by which the statements of case must be sent to the Inspectorate. Copies of the statement of case will be circulated to all the parties.

The timetable is as follows:[19]

(1) Within 8 weeks of the start date, the Planning Inspectorate must receive the local authority's statement of case and supporting documents. The statement of case is then sent by the Planning Inspectorate to the relevant parties and anyone who has made a written representation with information where the documents can be examined.

(2) Within 12 weeks of the start date, the Planning Inspectorate must receive from the recipients of the authority's statement of case their own statement of case. The Planning Inspectorate copies these to all the parties, including the local authority.

---

[18] See the Planning Inspectorate, 'The venue and facilities for public inquiries, hearings and examinations' (updated June 2017), available at www.gov.uk.

[19] Late material may be accepted if there are good reasons, such as ill health or a postal strike.

The next stage is for the inspector to make a site visit. Objectors can ask to accompany the inspector. If they do so, the local authority must also be present. If the inspector decides that an accompanied visit is necessary, the Planning Inspectorate will give at least 2 weeks' notice of the time and place it will take place.

The purpose of the site visit is for the inspector to see the order route and surrounding paths and to note the physical features. During the site visit, the inspector cannot discuss the arguments of either side.

If further evidence is sent to the inspector by an entirely new party after the deadlines but before he makes his decision, and it is material to the decision, he will send the evidence to everyone who has made written representations and give them the opportunity to reply. In extraordinary circumstances, late evidence may be accepted from a party who is already involved.

The authority must advertise the hearing in the local area, not less than 4 weeks before it is due to start. It must put notices at the ends of the relevant paths, in places where notices are usually displayed in the area and in at least one local newspaper. The notices must contain the date, time and place of the hearing, the section of the Act under which the order has been made, a description of the land to which the order relates, the effect of the order and where the documents relating to the hearing can be inspected.

The authority and objectors should send the Inspectorate a written statement of their case with accompanying documents at least 3 weeks before the date of the hearing. Copies of the statements and documents will be sent to the other parties. This is so that everyone can study the issues beforehand.

It may be that it will become clear in the pre-hearing procedure that a hearing is not appropriate. On other occasions, this may become apparent at the hearing itself. In either case, the inspector can decide that the hearing procedure be abandoned and a public inquiry held or that the matter should be dealt with by written representations.

9.7 Public inquiry

9.7.1 Introduction

Public inquiries relating to public rights of way are governed by the Rights of Way (Hearings and Inquiries Procedure) (England) Rules 2007.[20]

---

[20] (SI 2007/2008).

In practice, public inquiries follow the same format whether they are concerned with public path orders or modification orders. Anyone may attend and may be professionally represented or appear in person. Inquiries usually last 1 or 2 days, but can last much longer. The length varies on the amount of evidence and the number of people who wish to speak.

The Planning Inspectorate has produced a facility note for public inquiries and hearings which is available on its website.[21]

9.7.2 Date and place

The Planning Inspectorate writes to all objectors telling them of its proposal to hold a public inquiry. The authority will usually fix a date and a place for the inquiry with the Planning Inspectorate. The place is likely to be a village hall reasonably near the order route.

Once the date and the place have been agreed, the Planning Inspectorate gives written notice to the local authority, other relevant local authorities, the applicant and landowners and occupiers, relevant persons, prescribed organisations and anyone else who has made known their interest in the order. The notice will give the start date, the time and place of the inquiry, describe the land to which the order relates and the effect of the order. It must also specify where the documents can be inspected and the date by which the statements of case and proofs of evidence must be sent to the Inspectorate. Copies of the statement of case will be circulated to all the parties.

Where it is known in advance that certain dates will be impossible, it is worth contacting the local authority before a date is fixed and requesting that an inquiry should not be held at that time. Once notice has been given, dates are changed only in very exceptional circumstances.

The timetable[22] for submitting statements of case is as follows:

(1) Within 8 weeks of the start date, the Planning Inspectorate must receive the local authority's statement of case and supporting documents. The statement of case is then sent by the Planning Inspectorate to the relevant parties and anyone who has made a

---

21 See the Planning Inspectorate, 'The venue and facilities for public inquiries, hearings and examinations' (updated June 2017), available at www.gov.uk.

22 Late material may be accepted if there are good reasons, such as ill health or a postal strike. The inspector may allow alterations or additions to the statement of case and proof of evidence at the inquiry.

written representation with information where the documents can be examined.

(2) Within 14 weeks of the start date, the Planning Inspectorate must receive from the recipients of the authority's statement of case their own statement of case. The Planning Inspectorate copies these to all the parties, including the local authority.

(3) Not less than 4 weeks before the start date, proofs of evidence (or notice that a statement of case is to be regarded as proof of evidence) must be received by the Planning Inspectorate. Copies of these are circulated to all the parties.

9.7.3 Advertising the inquiry

The inquiry must be advertised by the authority in a local newspaper, and a notice put up at either end of each way affected by the order, as well as at a place where public notices are usually displayed in the district. This must be done at least 4 weeks before the inquiry is due to start.

The notices must contain the date, time and place of the inquiry, the section of the Act under which the order has been made, a description of the land to which the order relates, the effect of the order and where the documents relating to the inquiry can be inspected.

9.7.4 The inquiry

The inspector, appointed by the Secretary of State, decides the procedure at the inquiry.

The usual pattern is that he will introduce himself and explain when he intends to allow breaks in the proceedings. He will ask for the names of those who wish to speak. In practice, most inspectors allow those who do not give their names, or arrive late, to speak. Those who have to leave the inquiry early should inform the inspector so that he can arrange for them to be heard.

The inspector will pass around an attendance list for everyone to sign with their full address. He will also ask if there is any member of the press present.

He will usually start the proceedings by asking the authority to present its case for the order first, unless it no longer supports the order, when a supporter will present the case.

The authority may introduce witnesses who have proofs of evidence. Copies should be provided for the inspector and the objectors. The objectors may cross-examine the witnesses. However, the inspector may intervene if the questions are irrelevant or repetitive or if the process is being abused. The inspector, too, may question the witnesses. Normally, the supporters of the order will not be allowed to cross-examine their own side.

Other people who support the order will then be asked to speak. They must be prepared to be cross-examined.

The objectors will then present their case and call their witnesses. They, in turn, may be cross-examined by the supporters of the order.

Sometimes, unexpected questions are raised, and the other party may ask for an adjournment to consider them. The inspector will decide whether to allow an adjournment. Often it may be for a few minutes only. More rarely, it may be necessary to adjourn the inquiry to another date. The inspector will have to announce the date and place for the adjournment. In *Powell v Secretary of State for the Environment, Food and Rural Affairs*,[23] it was held on the particular facts that the refusal of an adjournment by the inspector amounted to a breach of natural justice.

Where there is no adjournment, the main objector will usually be given an opportunity of summing up the evidence of the objectors and making the relevant legal submissions on the evidence. Although, ideally, the legal submissions should be in writing, this is sometimes not possible as they may have emerged during the course of the inquiry. Inspectors will often ask for hand-written submissions and provide for copies to be made for the authority.

Lastly, the authority will make a closing statement which will probably deal with points raised by the objectors. The statement should not raise any new evidence. If, however, the authority suggests a modification to the order, the objectors will be given a chance to reply.

9.7.5 The site visit

Although the inspector will have visited the site before the inquiry, he will normally make another visit accompanied by at least one person supporting the order and one objecting. Anyone can accompany him, but he will not make the visit accompanied by one side alone. No new evidence can be given, but anyone may point out the physical features mentioned at the inquiry.

---

[23] [2009] EWHC 643 (Admin).

9.7.6 Evidence produced after the inquiry

Sometimes, evidence is given to the Planning Inspectorate after the inquiry, but before the inspector makes his decision. The evidence will be passed to him. If the inspector decides that new points have been raised which will affect his decision, he will send the evidence to anyone who presented their case or objected at the inquiry, giving them the chance to reply.

Where the Secretary of State is to make the decision, the evidence will be sent to him.

9.8 Substantive issues

9.8.1 General principles

Public rights of way generate a great deal of controversy. Many irrelevant points are likely to be aired at inquiries and hearings and indeed in written representations. Although inspectors tend to be extremely patient and tolerant, these irrelevant matters will not affect the decision. They merely prolong the procedures and in extreme cases may result in an order for costs.

9.8.2 Public path orders

Before confirming a public path order, the inspector has to ensure that the tests set out in the relevant section relating to the order are fulfilled. These are discussed in detail in Chapters 3 and 6.

For a creation order, an inspector must be satisfied that there is a need for a new path and that it is expedient to create one, taking into account the extent to which the path would add to the convenience or enjoyment of a substantial section of the public or those living in the area and any effect it would have on those with an interest in the land, after considering their entitlement to compensation.[24]

To extinguish a path, the inspector must be satisfied that it is expedient to do so having regard to the extent to which it appears to him the path would, apart from the order, be used by the public and the effect on the adjoining land of closing the path, taking into account the compensation provisions.[25] Obstructions which block the route are ignored in answering

---

24 HA 1980, s 26.

25 HA 1980, s 118.

these questions. In other words, the inspector considers how the path would be used if the obstructions were not there.

An inspector must not confirm a diversion order unless he is satisfied that the diverted path will not be substantially less convenient to the public and that it is expedient to confirm the order having regard to the public enjoyment of the path as a whole, the effect it would have on other land served by the existing public right of way and on the land over which the path is to be diverted, taking into account the compensation provisions.[26]

When considering concurrent orders for a public path creation order or diversion order and an extinguishment order, the inspector may consider whether the route is still needed after a new path is created or an existing path diverted. There is no provision, however, for creating or diverting a path on the basis that another path is extinguished. It therefore seems that the creation and diversion tests must be fulfilled independently before a decision can be made to extinguish a path.

In confirming a diversion or stopping-up order under the TCPA 1990, the inspector must be satisfied that the order is necessary for the development to be carried out.[27] He must also take into account in making his decision whether the advantages of a diversion or stopping up of the route outweigh the disadvantages.

Where the authority stops up a footpath or bridleway on its own land, the inspector must be sure that the authority has or will provide an alternative way or that such a way is not needed.[28]

9.8.3 Modification orders

Before confirming a definitive map order, the inspector has to consider whether or not the evidence supports the order. He is concerned only with ascertaining whether a public right of way exists and what is its status. He is not concerned with whether the path is wanted, nor with the effect it would have on amenity, security, privacy or the environment.

Unlike public path orders which change the status of public rights of way, modification orders are concerned only with ensuring that the definitive map and statement record accurately the existing position.

---

26 HA 1980, s 119. See *R (Young) v Secretary of State for the Environment, Food and Rural Affairs* [2002] EWHC 844 (Admin) for the separate tests that must be fulfilled.

27 TCPA 1990, s 259.

28 TCPA 1990, s 258.

9.8.4 Evidence relating to modification

In confirming or otherwise modification orders, the inspector bases his decision on evidence. This may be documentary or user evidence or, as is usual, a combination of the two. It is seldom that the evidence is clear-cut. The highway authority and objectors are likely to interpret the documents in different ways.

User evidence is evidence of the use by the public of the routes covered by the order. It may include declarations, written statements or oral evidence. Obviously, if witnesses appear at the inquiry and give evidence which may be subject to cross-examination, their evidence will carry more weight.

9.8.5 The decision

Most orders are decided by an inspector on behalf of the Secretary of State. Where the decision is particularly important or sensitive, the Secretary of State may call in the decision and make it himself.

The inspector will send his decision in a letter to the authority. The letter will describe the physical features of the path, set out the main arguments of the authority and the objectors and give his conclusions and decision. Copies of the letter will be sent to the local authority, the applicant, objectors and to other people who have requested a copy.

If the Secretary of State has called in the decision, he will consider the inspector's report and recommendations but does not necessarily follow them. He will give his decision in a letter to the authority. Copies will be sent to the same people as would receive a copy had the decision been made by an inspector.

The decision, whether made by the inspector or Secretary of State, will be to confirm the order, refuse to confirm the order or to confirm the order with modifications.

Certain modifications have to be re-advertised. Where a public path order or definitive map order is modified and the modification involves moving the line of the path or widening it, such changes must be advertised. In addition, a modified definitive map order which shows a new path, deletes all or part of a path or changes the status of a path in an order must be advertised.[29] Where a public right of way for mechanically propelled vehicles has been established but those rights are extinguished by section 67 of the NERCA 2006, the Secretary of State should confirm

---

29 HA 1980, Sch 6, para 2(3); WLCA 1981, Sch 15, para 8.

the order as a restricted byway. As the status of the path has been changed, notice of the proposal to change the order should be advertised.[30]

Objections can be made to the advertised modified order and, if these are not withdrawn, there will have to be another inquiry unless the parties agree to proceed by written representations or a hearing.

The Planning Inspectorate has given the following advice as to objections or representations which may be heard at a second or subsequent public inquiry or hearing:[31]

> (i) Where objections or representations are made that only relate to the proposed modification(s)
>
> Those making such objections or representations have the right to be heard (at a public inquiry or hearing), if they wish to exercise this right. On some occasions it might be possible to proceed to the Inspector's final decision on the basis of written submissions should the parties consent. The Inspector will only be able to consider evidence which relates to his proposed modification(s), and cannot consider evidence which is not related to the proposed modification(s).
>
> (ii) Where evidence is submitted or submissions are made at a second inquiry[32] or hearing, that do not relate to the proposed modification(s)
>
> Should anyone ask to give evidence that relates to an unmodified part of the order, the Inspector should not hear it at the second inquiry. Instead, he/she should advise them to set out their evidence in writing to the Planning Inspectorate (within a reasonable time scale) and continue to hear the evidence which is relevant to the proposed modification.
>
> If new evidence relating to the unmodified part of the order is received, the Inspector will decide how the new evidence ought appropriately to be dealt with which may lead, for example, to the re-opening the original inquiry[33] or hearing.
>
> (iii) Where there is a mixture of objections or representations some of which relate and others which do not relate to the proposed modification(s)
>
> Depending on the issues raised, it may be necessary to hold a joint inquiry into both the unmodified and modified parts of the order. However, in relation to the unmodified part of the order, the Inspector cannot

---

30 WLCA 1981, Sch 15, para 8(2)(a), (b) and (c).

31 The Planning Inspectorate, Rights of way advice note 10, 'Inquiries and hearings into proposed modifications' (Revised November 2014), available at www.gov.uk.

32 Held under WLCA 1981, Sch 15, para 8(2); HA 1980, Sch 6, para 2(3); and TCPA 1990, Sch 14, para 3(6).

33 Held under WLCA 1981, Sch 15, para 7(2); HA 1980, Sch 6, para 2(2); and TCPA 1990, Sch 14, para 3(3).

reconsider evidence which has already been heard or presented: the evidence must be new.

(iv) Where there are objections or representations that do not relate to the proposed modification

The Inspector will consider what the appropriate course of action is to take – that is, whether to re-open the original inquiry or hearing, deal with the matter by way of written representations or not invite any further comments. Where an inquiry or hearing is held, the Inspector will only be able to consider new evidence which relates to the unmodified part of the order. The Inspector cannot consider evidence which has already been heard or presented, nor can he consider evidence which relates to the proposed modifications. If anyone at the inquiry or hearing asks to give evidence relating to the modified part of the order, the Inspector should advise them to set out their evidence in writing to the Planning Inspectorate (within a reasonable time scale) and continue to hear the evidence which is relevant to the unmodified part of the order.

This advice is based on the Planning Inspectorate's interpretation of *Marriott v Secretary of State or the Environment, Transport and the Regions*.[34]

9.9 Costs[35]

The costs of determining a contested order where there is a public inquiry or hearing can be recovered by the Secretary of State. He can also do so where he appoints someone to deal with the matter by written representations.[36] The parties in rights of way proceedings when an order is submitted for determination to the Planning Inspectorate usually bear their own costs.

There is no power to award that costs be paid by the other side where the written representations procedure is followed. Where there is a public inquiry or a hearing[37] and an order is confirmed under the TCPA 1990 or the WLCA 1981 or under the HA 1980, costs may be awarded where one party has behaved unreasonably, frivolously or in a vexatious manner.[38] For instance, if the inspector holds that the order is

34 [2000] EWHC 652 (Admin).

35 See Defra, Rights of Way Circular 1/09, 'Guidance for Local Authorities' (Defra, 2009).

36 HA 1980, Sch 6, para 2B(4) (not yet in force). Inserted by DA 2015, s 25(6).

37 CROWA 2000, Sch 5, para 11(8) adds para 10A to WLCA 1981, Sch 15 with the effect that Local Government Act 1972, s 250(2)–(5) applies to hearings as well as public inquiries.

38 See Department for Communities and Local Government, Circular 03/09, 'Costs Awards in Appeals and Other Planning Proceedings' (6 April 2009).

fundamentally defective, the authority may have to pay the objector's costs. Another example is where the evidence shows that the local authority should not have made an order in the first place.[39] Objectors who persist in irrelevant objections may be held to have behaved unreasonably and be ordered to pay the authority's costs. An objector who requests an inquiry and fails to turn up or appoint someone to represent him may be liable for costs. Failure to comply with the Rights of Way (Hearings and Inquiries) (England) Rules 2007[40] may also result in an order for costs being made against the defaulter.

Creation orders under the HA 1980 are similar to compulsory purchase orders. If they are confirmed, they will take away some of the landowner's interests in his land. The landowner is entitled to compensation. He may also be entitled to compensation where there is a diversion or extinguishment order. Such orders are known as analogous orders (analogous to compulsory purchase orders). If a landowner makes a successful objection to an analogous order at a public inquiry, his costs will automatically be paid by the authority.[41]

Applications for costs should be made after the authority has made its closing statement, but before the public inquiry has been officially closed. The inspector will give the other side a chance to counter the claim. A report will be made to the Secretary of State on the application for costs. He will decide whether to award costs.

Normally, applications for costs cannot be made after the inquiry has closed. The inspector should make this clear at the start of the inquiry. Where there is a good reason for a late application, this should be made to the Planning Inspectorate. If the application is accepted, both sides will be asked to make written representations before the Secretary of State makes his decision.

9.10 Challenging the decision

9.10.1 Statutory review

Where the inspector has confirmed the order, an application may be made to the High Court challenging the decision on the ground that the decision is not within the powers of the inspector or that the proper procedures

---

39 *R v Secretary of State ex parte Smith and Deller* [1995] JPL 42 (inspector's decision not to award costs quashed on judicial review).

40 (SI 2007/2008).

41 Local Authorities (Recovery of Costs for Public Path Orders) Regulations 1993 (SI 1993/407).

have not been followed and, as a consequence, the claimant's interests have been substantially prejudiced. The application must be made within 42 days of the decision being published in the newspaper. From the time an order is made, the decision may not be challenged in any other legal proceedings whatsoever.[42]

In *R (Elveden Farms Ltd) v Secretary of State for Environment and Rural Affairs*,[43] the judge quashed the decision of the inspector rather than the order itself.[44]

9.10.2 Judicial review

Where the inspector refuses to confirm an order, an application may be made for leave for judicial review. Judicial review proceedings must be brought without delay and, in any event, within 3 months of the decision.

In order to succeed on judicial review, it will be necessary to show that the inspector has acted totally unreasonably or that there has been a mistake of law.

A judicial review is neither an appeal nor an opportunity for re-running the evidence.

9.11 Complaints

9.11.1 The Planning Inspectorate

A person who is dissatisfied with the inspector or the way the order is being handled by Defra may write to the Planning Inspectorate. However, the only way to challenge a decision of the inspector is by a statutory or judicial review.

9.11.2 The Parliamentary Commissioner for Administration (the Ombudsman)

Complaints about the Planning Inspectorate or the inspector may be made to the Ombudsman through an MP. He cannot, however, alter or

---

42 HA 1980, Sch 2, para 4; WLCA 1981, Sch 15, para 12. *R v Cornwall County Council ex parte Huntington* [1994] 1 All ER 694.

43 [2012] EWHC 644 (Admin).

44 Cf *Jones v Welsh Assembly Government* [2008] EWHC 3515 (Admin), where both the inspector's decision and the order were quashed.

question the decision. He is not concerned with the merits of the case, but with the administration procedure.

9.11.3 The Council on Tribunals

Complaints about the basic procedure in processing an order can be made to the Council on Tribunals.

9.11.4 The Local Ombudsman

Complaints about the way the authority handled the order may be made to the Local Ombudsman. He cannot, however, question the merits of the order or change the decision.

9.11.5 The Planning Inspectorate Guidance on Public Rights of Way

Information formerly on the Planning Inspectorate website is now to be found on the general government website. The information is updated from time to time.

The information in the consistency guidelines and advice notes is useful not only to inspectors and local authorities, but also to those who are contesting orders. It is important to know what guidance the inspector is following even if it is considered that the guidance, which does not have the force of law, is wrong.

Particularly useful are the guidance and guidelines referred to below:

- 'Guidance on procedures for considering objections to definitive map and public path orders in England' (October 2018), www.gov.uk/government/uploads/system/uploads/attachment_data/file/498135/Row_Booklet_revised_January_2016.pdf.
- 'Definitive map orders: consistency guidelines' (April 2003), www.gov.uk/government/uploads/system/uploads/attachment_data/file/435666/consistency_guide.pdf.
- Rights of way advice notes, www.gov.uk/government/collections/rights-of-way-advice-notes.

10 Natural England: Diversions for Sites of Special Scientific Interest and Coastal Access

10.1 Sites of special scientific interest diversion orders

Natural England or Natural Resources Wales may apply to the local highway authority for a diversion order for the protection of an SSSI.[1] The council's powers to make a diversion order extend to footpaths, bridleways, restricted byways (whether on the definitive map or not) and such paths if shown on the definitive map, but over which the public have a right of way for vehicular and all other kinds of traffic. The highway authority may also divert highways shown on the definitive map as BOATs, but not a highway which is a trunk or special road.

The highway must be in, or form part of, or be adjacent to, or be contiguous with an SSSI. The test for making the order is that the public use of the highway is causing or is likely to cause significant damage to the flora, fauna or geological or physiographical features which caused the area to be designated an SSSI and it is expedient in order to prevent such damage that the whole or part of the path should be diverted.

An SSSI diversion order must not divert the cul-de-sac end of a highway, nor where the termination is on a highway, otherwise than to another point on the same highway or a highway connected with it.

Before deciding to make the order, the council may require Natural England or Natural Resources Wales to pay or make a contribution to any compensation payable to a third party, or costs which may be

---

1 HA 1980, s 119D, inserted by CROWA 2000, Sch 6, Pt I, para 12.

incurred in bringing the new route into a condition fit for public use, or any costs due to another highway authority for work carried out.

An application must be made on a prescribed form and be accompanied by a map on a prescribed scale.[2] The map must show the line of the existing path and the proposed new route. The map must indicate whether it is proposed to create a new right of way over the whole of the new site or whether some of it is already comprised in a footpath or bridleway. The application must also have an assessment in the prescribed form of the effects of the public right of way on the SSSI.

At least 14 days before an application is made, notice in the prescribed form must be given by Natural England or Natural Resources Wales to any owner, lessee or occupier of land over which the old or new route would run, and to such other persons as may be prescribed. Schedule 6 to the HA 1980 will govern the making, confirmation, validity and date of operation of the orders. The council, in deciding whether it is expedient to make, and the council or Secretary of State, in deciding whether it is expedient to confirm, an order, must consider whether the damage could be prevented by the council making a road traffic regulation order and whether such an order would cause less inconvenience to the public than a diversion order. Where an SSSI diversion order is made by the Secretary of State, on the failure of the council to do so, he must have regard to the same considerations.

An order will not be confirmed unless the Secretary of State, or the council for an unopposed order, is satisfied that the tests for making the order have been fulfilled and that it is expedient to confirm the order having regard to the effect the diversion will have on the enjoyment of the public right of way as a whole, and the effect that the diversion will have on any other land served by the existing right of way and the land over which the new route will run, taking into account provisions for compensation.

The new route may be unconditional or subject to limitations and conditions, even if the old route was not.

The new route will come into existence, and the old route will be extinguished, on the date specified in the order. However, where work is necessary on the new route, the old route will not be extinguished until the council certifies that the work has been carried out. There is

---

2 HA 1980, s 119E, as amended by NERCA 2006, s 105(2), Sch 11, para 65, Sch 12. See the Highways (SSSI Diversion Orders) (England) Regulations 2007 (SI 2007/1494) for the procedure, forms and notices.

no obligation imposed on a highway authority to provide, on any highway created by an SSSI diversion order, a metalled carriageway.

The Secretary of State may make a diversion order, even though the conservation authority (Natural England or Natural Resources Wales) has not made an application for an order to the highway authority.[3] Where it does make an application but the council has neither confirmed the order nor submitted it to the Secretary of State for confirmation within 6 months of receiving the application, the Secretary of State may make the diversion order without consulting the council.[4] Before making an order, the Secretary of State may require the conservation body to enter into an agreement with the council to pay or contribute to any compensation payable or any expenses in relation to making up the new path.[5]

10.2 Coastal access

10.2.1 Introduction

The MCAA 2009 introduces a new right of access to the coast for the public to enjoy open-air recreation on foot. The Act imposes a coastal access duty on the Secretary of State and Natural England. The legislation is being implemented by Natural England proposing a series of long-distance paths around the coast[6] of England using the powers conferred by the NPACA 1949, as amended by the MCAA 2009. After consultation with local people and the relevant access authorities, a report on the proposed routes is made to the Secretary of State.[7] Once approved and any necessary physical works completed, access is available from a date specified in an order made by the Secretary of State under section 2(1) of the CROWA 2000 or under any other enactments which provide for public access.

This is complex legislation, as, in order to achieve its aim, the MCAA 2009 incorporates sections 50 to 55 of the NPACA 1949 and inserts new sections (namely, sections 50A to 50G) into that Act, and modifies and inserts a new section 3A into the CROWA 2000. The definition of

3 HA 1980, s 120(3C).

4 HA 1980, s 120(3D).

5 HA 1980, s 120(7).

6 For the definition of 'coast', see MCAA 2009, s 300. Coast includes non-excluded islands. For treatment of estuaries, see MCAA 2009, s 301.

7 See 'Coastal Access – Natural England's Approved Scheme 2013 (NE446)', http://publications.naturalengland.org.uk/publication/5327964912746496.

'coastal land' is contained in a statutory instrument,[8] which also introduces further modifications to the CROWA 2000.

10.2.2 The English coastal route

The MCAA 2009 imposes a duty on Natural England and the Secretary of State to secure one or more long-distance routes for the whole of the English coast (the English coastal route) along which the public may make recreational journeys on foot or by ferry and which passes over land that is accessible to the public (except to the extent that it is completed by ferry).[9] The ferry does not have to be operating at all times of the day or year. A person is regarded as able to make a journey by ferry even if the operation of the ferry is seasonal.[10]

Land accessible to the public by virtue of section 2(1) of the CROWA 2000 fulfils the coastal access duty if it is coastal margin, even if it is subject to exclusions or restrictions,[11] but not if it is other access land under that Act. This is because the management regime for coastal margin land is different in some respects from open country and registered common land which is not coastal margin.

Land which is accessible to the public under section 193 of the Law of Property Act 1925, the Commons Act 1899, Part V of the NPACA 1949 or the Ancient Monuments and Archaeological Areas Act 1979 does not count as access land under the CROWA 2000. Although it counts as accessible to the public for purposes of the coastal access duty[12] and so forms part of the coastal margin, coastal access rights do not apply. Access will be according to the provisions of the particular statute.

The third category of land which is treated as accessible to the public for this purpose is land which is excepted land under Schedule 1 to the CROWA 2000, but which is accessible to the public by virtue of any enactment or rule of law.[13] For instance, a new category of excepted land has been introduced where the land is coastal margin if the land is, or forms part of, a highway.[14] Access will be by virtue of the highway rights and not under section 2(1) of the CROWA 2000. This is so that there are

---

8 Access to the Countryside (Coastal Margin) (England) Order 2010 (SI 2010/558).

9 MCAA 2009, s 296(1) and (2). See NPACA 1949, ss 53 and 55G for the provision of ferries.

10 MCAA 2009, s 296(7).

11 MCAA 2009, s 296(5)(a).

12 MCAA 2009, s 296(5)(b).

13 MCAA 2009, s 296(5)(c).

14 CROWA 2000, Schs 1 and 13B.

not two different sets of rules applicable to highways. However, military land where access might be permitted by a bylaw[15] (although excepted land under Schedule 1) does not count as accessible to the public.

10.2.3 Coastal margin

The English coastal route comes within the definition of coastal margin. But in addition, Natural England and the Secretary of State are under a duty to secure in association with the English coastal route a margin of land along the length of the English coast accessible to the public for enjoyment by them in conjunction with the route or otherwise, unless the land is excepted land. Coastal margin will include areas such as beaches, cliffs, rocks and dunes. The margin does not have to be accessed directly from the English coastal route. Access may be obtained, for instance, from a public right of way or from land on which the public have access under other legislation.

'Accessible to the public' has the same meaning as has been set out in relation to the English coastal route. However, Natural England and the Secretary of State are under a duty to secure access under section 3A of the CROWA 2000 only. Although land may be accessible to the public under other enactments, Natural England and the Secretary of State are not under a duty as far as the coastal margin, other than the English coastal route, is concerned to extend access by other means.[16]

10.2.4 Considerations in discharging the duty

In discharging this duty, Natural England must have regard to:[17]

(a) the safety and convenience of those using the English coastal route,

(b) the desirability of that route adhering to the periphery of the coast and providing views of the sea, and

(c) the desirability of ensuring that so far as reasonably practicable interruptions to that route are kept to a minimum.

Natural England must also aim to strike a fair balance between the interests of the public and the interests of any person with a fee simple or a leasehold interest in, or who is in lawful occupation of, the land.[18]

---

15 Under Military Lands Act 1892, s 14 or Military Lands Act 1900, s 2.

16 MCAA 2009, s 296(6).

17 MCAA 2009, s 297(1) and (2).

18 MCAA 2009, s 297(3) and (4).

10.2.5 Time scale in discharging the duty

The establishment of the routes and coastal margins is being carried out in stages. Natural England envisage the process will be completed in 2020. However, there is not a cut-off date for completing the work. Natural England does not have to act to a specified timetable and can decide which areas should have priority depending on the existing available access.[19]

The Natural England website[20] gives details of the progress which is being made on the implementation of the coastal routes and margins.

10.3 Definition of 'English coast'

10.3.1 Coast and islands

The 'English coast' means the coast in England adjacent to the sea and includes islands which are not excluded.[21] 'Not excluded' means islands which are accessible or islands specified by the Secretary of State in an order. An accessible island is one which can be reached on foot from the mainland of England or from another island (other than an excluded island) across the foreshore or by a bridge, tunnel or causeway, even if it is possible to do so only at certain times. The means of access to an accessible island is regarded as part of the English coast. The Secretary of State can specify an island only where the coast is long enough to enable the public to make an extensive journey on foot.

10.3.2 Estuaries

The MCAA 2009 provides that Natural England may treat estuaries as if they were the sea.[22] The area of the estuary for the purposes of the statute is:

(a) the waters from the seaward limit of the estuarial waters of the river upstream to the first public foot crossing, or

(b) if Natural England so decides, the waters from the seaward limit of the estuarial waters of the river upstream to such limit, downstream of the first public foot crossing, as may be specified by it.

---

19 See MCAA 2009, s 296(4).

20 See www.gov.uk/government/collections/england-coast-path-improving-public-access-to-the-coast.

21 MCAA 2009, s 300.

22 MCAA 2009, s 301.

'First public foot crossing' means a bridge or tunnel with a public right of way.

When exercising its functions, Natural England must have regard to: (1) the nature of the land; (2) the topography of the shoreline adjacent to the estuary; (3) the width of the river; (4) the recreational benefit to the public of coastal access being extended to the estuary; (5) the extent to which the land bordering those waters would, if it were coastal margin, be excepted land; (6) whether it is desirable to continue the English coastal route to a particular physical feature (whether of the landscape or otherwise) or viewpoint; and (7) the existence of a ferry by which the public may cross the river.

Natural England and the Secretary of State must also comply with the requirements set out at 10.2.4 regarding the discharge of its coastal access duty. The Secretary of State may make a different decision from Natural England on whether waters of a river are to be treated as part of the sea.

10.4 Definition of 'coastal margin'

Section 3 of the CROWA 2000 as originally enacted contained a power for the Secretary of State (as respects England) or the National Assembly (as respects Wales) to amend by order the definition of open country so as to include coastal land. Coastal land is defined as the foreshore or land adjacent to the foreshore (including in particular any cliff, bank, barrier, dune, beach or flat which is adjacent to the foreshore). This section has now been amended so that it applies to Wales only, with the reference to the National Assembly being replaced by 'Welsh Ministers'.[23]

A new section, section 3A, has been inserted into the CROWA 2000. This allows the Secretary of State to make an order defining coastal margin in England. Any order must be approved by resolution of each House of Parliament. The Access to the Countryside (Coastal Margin) (England) Order 2010[24] made under this provision came into effect on 6 April 2010.

Land is coastal margin if it falls within one of four descriptions:[25]

---

23 MCAA 2009, s 303(4).

24 (SI 2010/558).

25 Access to the Countryside (Coastal Margin) (England) Order 2010 (SI 2010/558), art 3.

(1) Land over which the line of an approved section of the English coastal route[26] passes and land which is adjacent to and within 2 metres either side. It also includes land to the seaward side of the 2 metres to the extremity off the foreshore. The land taken as a whole must be coastal land as described in section 3 of the CROWA 2000.[27]

(2) Land which is on the landward side of the English coastal route which is foreshore, cliff, bank, barrier, dune, beach or flat or land which is accessible to the public under the Law of Property Act 1925 the Commons Act 1899, the NPACA 1949 and the Ancient Monuments and Archaeological Areas Act 1979.[28] This land, when taken together with the approved section, must be coastal land.

(3) Land over which the line of an official alternative route passes and adjacent land within 2 metres either side of that line.

(4) Land over which a temporary route passes and adjacent land within 2 metres either side of that line provided it is land over which the owner has agreed the temporary route may pass.[29]

Where a route is subject to coastal erosion and there are provisions in the report allowing the route to roll back, the references to the approved section of the coastal route are references to the line of the section as it has effect from time to time.[30]

Proposals in the report may allow the landward boundary of the relevant coastal margin to coincide with a physical feature even if it includes land which would not otherwise be coastal margin or excludes coastal land from being coastal margin.[31]

If there are proposals in the report for an alternative route, the references to an official alternative route refer to the line of the route as

---

26 'Approved section of English coastal route' means a route in relevant approved proposals (other than an official alternative route): Access to the Countryside (Coastal Margin) (England) Order 2010 (SI 2010/558), art 2.

27 I.e. the foreshore or land adjacent to the foreshore (including in particular any cliff, bank, barrier, dune, beach or flat which is adjacent to the foreshore).

28 CROWA 2000, s 15.

29 I.e. the land is within NPACA 1949, s 55I(4)(d).

30 Access to the Countryside (Coastal Margin) (England) Order 2010 (SI 2010/558), art 4.

31 Access to the Countryside (Coastal Margin) (England) Order 2010 (SI 2010/558), art 5.

it has effect from time to time in accordance with the relevant approved proposals.[32] And, if the proposals so provide, the landward or seaward side of the alternative route strip[33] will coincide with the physical feature identified in the proposal.

10.5 Excepted land

Access rights do not apply to excepted land. The categories of excepted land set out in Schedule 1 to the CROWA 2000 have been modified to take account of coastal access.[34] The following categories are the same as for open country and registered common land: land which is (1) covered by buildings or the curtilage of such land; (2) used as a park or garden; (3) used as a railway or tramway; (4) covered by pens for temporary detention of livestock; (5) used as a racecourse or aerodrome; (6) being developed and which will then qualify under certain other excepted categories; (7) covered by works for an electronic communications code network and the curtilage thereof; and (8) regulated under section 14 of the Military Lands Act 1892 and section 2 of the Military Lands Act 1900.

Land covered by works for statutory undertakings and the curtilage thereof is excepted land, but in the case of coastal margin, land is not excepted if the works are sea or flood defence works. Land used for the getting of minerals by surface working, including quarrying, is excepted land, but where the land is coastal margin, the land will not be excepted where sand or gravel are removed from the beach or foreshore in pursuance of a legal right.

Four categories of excepted land may be subject to an access strip. This will normally be the line of the route and 2 metres either side. It may be that the width is wider or narrower in order for the boundary to coincide with a physical feature. The categories are: land on which the soil is being, or at any time within the previous 12 months has been, disturbed by any ploughing or drilling for the planting or sowing of crops or trees; land used as a golf course; land which is, or forms part of, a regulated

---

[32] Access to the Countryside (Coastal Margin) (England) Order 2010 (SI 2010/558), art 6.

[33] This means the land which becomes coastal margin during the operation of that route: Access to the Countryside (Coastal Margin) (England) Order 2010 (SI 2010/558).

[34] By Access to the Countryside (Coastal Margin) (England) Order 2010 (SI 2010/558), Sch 1.

caravan or camp site;[35] and land which is or forms part of a burial ground. The last two categories are not excepted land for access land other than coastal margin.

Two other categories of excepted land apply to coastal margin access land only, namely land which is, or forms part of, a school playing field or is otherwise used or occupied by the school and land which is a highway. There is no provision for an access strip, although in the case of a highway, there will be highway rights of access.

10.6 Natural England's Approved Scheme

The MCAA 2009[36] imposed a duty on Natural England to prepare a scheme setting out the approach it would take in discharging its coastal access duty. The scheme had to be submitted to the Secretary of State within 12 months of the section coming into force. The Secretary of State had to lay a copy of the scheme before Parliament, and it was approved on 23 March 2010. Natural England may review the scheme at any time, but must do so within 3 years.[37] Version 2 of the scheme was approved by the Secretary of State on 9 July 2013.[38] The report of each review must be published as soon as possible after each review. In discharging the access duty, Natural England must act in accordance with the Approved Scheme.[39]

The scheme explains the basis on which Natural England will make reports to the Secretary of State on the extent and management of coastal access. Natural England will divide the coast into stretches, each of which will be the subject of a separate coastal access report to the Secretary of State. The reports will include recommendations on the English coastal route and coastal margin and any exclusions and restrictions on access and other management options. Where an existing route along the coast complies with the criteria in the scheme, Natural England is likely to adopt that route. If there is no such route or an existing route is unsatisfactory, a new or improved route will be suggested. Existing

35 For meaning of regulated camp site, see Access to the Countryside (Coastal Margin) (England) Order 2010 (SI 2010/558), Sch 1, para 9(f).

36 MCAA 2009, s 298.

37 MCAA 2009, s 299(2).

38 'Coastal Access – Natural England's Approved Scheme 2013 (NE446)', http://publications.naturalengland.org.uk/publication/5327964912746496.

39 MCAA 2009, s 298(10).

National Trails may be modified.[40] However, no existing public rights of way will be removed.

In the scheme, Natural England uses the term 'trail' to describe the line on the map over which the long-distance route passes and the 2 metres on either side. 'Spreading room' is the term used to describe any land, other than the trail, which forms part of the coastal margin and has public rights of access. Such rights may be coastal access rights under the CROWA 2000 or rights under the legislation set out in section 15 of that Act. Each report will contain an indication of the spreading room by maps and/or description.

Part A of the scheme sets out the background, the statutory framework and the implementation process. Part B of the scheme considers the key principles of alignment and management, taking into account the interests of the public and the owners/occupiers and how Natural England intends to strike the appropriate balance between these interests. Part C illustrates how the key principles are to be applied. It discusses the various types of land cover and land forms.

10.7 Preparation of reports

10.7.1 English coastal route

The NPACA 1949 gives Natural England a power to prepare and submit to the Secretary of State a report proposing a long-distance path.[41] Certain requirements are set out in section 51(2) of the Act. A report must contain a map showing the route and indicating where on the route there is an existing right of way, and proposals for: (1) the maintenance and improvement of such rights of way; (2) the provision and improvement of any new public paths as may be required; (3) the provision and operation of ferries where they are needed; and also (4) the provision of accommodation, meals and refreshments along the route.

However, for the purposes of the coastal access duty, Natural England may prepare a report regardless of whether those requirements are fulfilled.[42] It is immaterial whether the route or any part of it is already a route in approved proposals relating to a long-distance route. The existing route might not in particular circumstances be sufficient to discharge the coastal access duty.

---

40 Under NPACA 1949, s 55.

41 NPACA 1949, s 55A, inserted by MCAA 2009, s 302.

42 NPACA 1949, s 55A(1).

Where Natural England considers it necessary or expedient to carry out an activity to facilitate the preparation of a report, it must consider whether it is appropriate for an access authority to do the work and, if so, it must take all reasonable steps to enter into an agreement with the authority.

10.7.2 Consultation[43]

Before preparing a report for a long-distance route, Natural England has to consult every National Park authority, joint planning board, county council, county borough council, district council, London borough council and local access forum through whose area the affected land is situated. These bodies must provide Natural England with such information as it may require for purposes of the report. Natural England must also consult any owner, lessee or licensee of the affected land.

'Affected land' means land over which the route, or any alternative route,[44] passes and any other land which is relevant coastal margin, or an alternative route strip of such alternative route, which is not excepted land.

Natural England must consult the Historic Buildings and Monuments Commission for England where the preservation of any monument, structure, work, site, garden or area of historic, architectural, traditional, artistic or archaeological interest may be affected, and the Environment Agency where there are issues of flood defence, coastal erosion or encroachment by the sea.

Where the interests of defence or national security may be affected, Natural England must consult the Secretary of State, who must provide Natural England with information on any exclusion or restriction of the right of access he proposes to make under section 28 of the CROWA 2000. He must notify Natural England if any of the information should not be disclosed on the ground of defence or national security.

10.7.3 Erosion of route

Where Natural England considers that the route passes through an area which is subject to significant coastal erosion or encroachment by the sea or other geomorphological processes, the report may contain proposals for the route to be determined by those proposals rather than as shown on the map. It may in particular provide for the route to be determined by

---

43 NPACA 1949, s 55D.

44 See 10.4 and NPACA 1949, s 55J.

reference to the edge of a cliff or boundary of a field. Natural England should consult the Environment Agency when drawing up the proposals.

The map which must accompany the report[45] must show the route as determined, at the time the report is prepared, in accordance with the proposals.[46]

10.7.4 Alternative routes

The report may include alternative routes which will operate as diversions during specified periods and any period when the ordinary route is closed due to a direction excluding access made under Chapter II of Part I of the CROWA 2000.[47] The normal route might be unsuitable for use due to flooding, high tide, coastal erosion or encroachment by the sea or the effect of a landslide.

Specified periods may be determined in accordance with the proposal, or by a person specified in the proposal, or by a person determined in accordance with the proposal, details of whom are notified to Natural England in accordance with the proposal. An example given in the Explanatory Notes accompanying the MCAA 2009 is an alternative route which will come into operation when a particular breed of bird starts to nest. As the time is likely to vary from year to year, the alternative route may come into effect when the warden notifies Natural England and puts up a sign stating that the alternative route should now be used.

The provisions of section 51(2) (setting out what must be included in a report proposing a long-distance route) and section 55B (rolling back of route where coastal erosion) of the NPACA 1949 apply to the alternative route.

10.7.5 Boundaries of coastal margin

The proposals in a report may provide for the landward side of the coastal margin to coincide with a physical feature.[48] This may mean that land which would otherwise be coastal margin is excluded or land which not is included. Where there is an alternative route, or an area is excluded from excepted land, the proposals may recommend that landward or seaward boundary should coincide with a physical boundary.

45 NPACA 1949, s 51(2).

46 NPACA 1949, s 55B.

47 NPACA 1949, s 55C.

48 NPACA 1949, s 55D.

The report must contain a map or a description sufficient to identify the landward boundary of the coastal margin. Natural England must on request supply an owner, occupier or licensee with a copy of the map.

10.7.6 Exclusions and restrictions

The report must set out any proposed exclusions and restrictions of access to the coastal margin.[49] These may also be imposed subsequently when the trail and spreading room are in operation for a particular section of the coast. They apply only where the rights of access are under the CROWA 2000.

Except for the purposes of defence and national security, when the relevant authority is the Ministry of Defence or the Home Office, respectively, Natural England is the sole relevant authority for giving directions on exclusions and restrictions relating to coastal access rights. It is clear from Natural England's Approved Scheme that directions will be relied on only as a last resort where alignment of the route or other management measures will be ineffective to deal with any problems.

Directions are similar to those which apply to other access land under the CROWA 2000. They may be given for the purposes of land management, public safety, fire prevention, nature conservation and heritage preservation. However, there are some differences. An exclusion or restriction on coastal access land for fire risk cannot exclude access along the trail, i.e. the line of the approved section of the English coastal route, or an official alternative or temporary route, and adjacent land 2 metres either side of the line.[50]

The 28-day exclusion at the discretion of the landowner does not apply to access land which is coastal margin.[51] Nor does the exclusion relating to dogs on grouse moors or on land used for lambing apply.[52] On the other hand, there is a specific category which applies only to coastal margin. A direction for an exclusion or restriction may be made where the land is salt marsh or mudflats which are unsuitable for public access.[53] An exclusion or restriction on coastal margin land for land management may be made by the relevant authority whether or not an application has been made by the person interested in the land.

---

49 NPACA 1949, s 55D(5).

50 CROWA 2000, s 25(1A).

51 CROWA 2000, s 22(9).

52 CROWA 2000, s 23(5).

53 CROWA 2000, s 25A.

If the approved proposals include restrictions or exclusions, they must be put in place. However, Natural England may subsequently vary or revoke them.[54]

10.7.7 Ferries

Natural England may include a proposal for a ferry as part of its coastal access duty to provide the English coastal route. The ferry does not have to be operating at all times of the day or year. A person is regarded as able to make a journey by ferry even if the operation of the ferry is seasonal.[55] The NPACA 1949[56] enables ferries to be provided and operated (or caused to be provided and operated) by the highway authority, or authorities, for the highways which the ferry will connect. Where the approach route is over access land which is not a highway, the power is vested in the highway authority responsible for that area.[57]

10.7.8 Consideration of coastal access reports

Natural England must advertise[58] a coastal access report and take reasonable steps to give notice[59] of the report to those who hold a 'relevant interest', i.e. a fee simple or leasehold interest or licence to occupy the land. Notice must also be given to each relevant access authority and local access forum, the Historic Buildings and Monuments Commission for England, the Environment Agency and the other persons specified in regulations.[60]

Any person with a relevant interest may make an objection to the report. Objections must be made with reasons on the grounds that the proposals in the report fail to strike a fair balance between the interests of the public and those with a relevant interest in the land with regard to proposals on:

---

54 NPACA 1949, s 55F.

55 MCAA 2009, s 296(7).

56 NPACA 1949, s 53.

57 NPACA 1949, s 55F.

58 NPACA 1949, Sch 1A, para 2(1)(a). Coastal Access Reports (Consideration and Modification Procedure) (England) Regulations 2010 (SI 2010/1976), reg 2.

59 NPACA 1949, Sch 1A, para 2(1)(b). Coastal Access Reports (Consideration and Modification Procedure) (England) Regulations 2010 (SI 2010/1976), reg 3.

60 NPACA 1949, Sch 1A, para 2(2). Coastal Access Reports (Consideration and Modification Procedure) (England) Regulations 2010 (SI 2010/1976), reg 3 and Sch 1 have specified: British Association for Shooting and Conservation, British Mountaineering Council, Country Land and Business Association, National Farmers Union, Open Spaces Society, Ramblers' Association, Royal Society for the Protection of Birds, Persons with sporting rights over the affected land.

(1) the position of the proposed route; (2) rollback of the route where there is erosion; (3) inclusion or failure to include alternative routes; (4) the inclusion or failure to include boundaries coinciding with physical features; (5) the inclusion of, or failure to include, exclusions and restrictions; or (6) the exercise or failure to exercise the discretions relating to estuaries.[61]

In order to remedy or mitigate the failure to strike a fair balance, objectors may propose modifications of the proposals provided they are practicable and take account of the safety and convenience of those using the route, the desirability of the route keeping to the coast and providing views of the sea with interruptions being kept to a minimum. Where the modification relates to an estuary in addition, regard must be had to the nature of the land, the shoreline and width of the river, the recreational benefit to the public, the extent of the excepted land, any particular physical feature or viewpoint and the existence of any ferry. The proposed modification must also be in accordance with Natural England's Approved or Revised Coastal Access Scheme.[62]

Objections received by Natural England must be forwarded to the Secretary of State.[63] The Secretary of State must in writing appoint a person (the appointed person) to consider whether an objection is admissible. Notice of the determination must be given to the objector, the Secretary of State and Natural England.[64]

Natural England must provide comments to the Secretary of State on any admissible objections. The appointed person may require Natural England to include information on any relevant alternative modifications of the proposals in the coastal access report, or an outline of any relevant rejected options considered by Natural England in the preparation of the coastal access report and its reasons for rejecting them, as well as any other relevant information.[65]

It is only those with relevant interests in the land who may make objections. However, any person may make a representation to Natural England about the report. Natural England must send representations made by any relevant access authority and local access forum, the

---

61 NPACA 1949, Sch 1A, para 3. Coastal Access Reports (Consideration and Modification Procedure) (England) Regulations 2010 (SI 2010/1976), reg 4 specifies how the objections and representations are to be made and the forms which must be used.

62 NPACA 1949, Sch 1A, para 3(5) and (6).

63 NPACA 1949, Sch 1A, para 4.

64 NPACA 1949, Sch 1A, paras 4 and 5.

65 NPACA 1949, Sch 1A, para 6.

Historic Buildings and Monuments Commission for England, the Environment Agency and other persons specified in the regulations to the Secretary of State.[66] Only a summary of representations made by others is required. Natural England must also send its comments on the representations.[67]

Where the appointed person has decided that there is an admissible objection, the Secretary of State must send him the relevant documents.[68] The appointed person may ask for other relevant information from Natural England or the Secretary of State.[69] He must then decide whether a fair balance has been struck in the proposals in the report on the matters specified in the objection.[70] If he is minded to hold that the proposals do not strike a fair balance, he must publish details of the objection with Natural England's comments, a statement that he is minded to determine that the proposals do not strike a fair balance, an invitation to submit to him representations about the objection, any relevant alternative modifications contained in Natural England's comments and any of his own comments on alternative modifications made by the objector or Natural England. Copies of the notice must be sent to the bodies mentioned in the previous paragraph, as well as those with a relevant interest and those who would have a relevant interest if the modifications took effect.[71]

On the other hand, if the appointed person considers that the proposals in the report do strike a fair balance, no further representations may be made. This is because there was an opportunity to make representations on Natural England's proposals before the determination.

The appointed person must give to the Secretary of State a report with reasons on his determination. If he concludes that the proposals do not strike a fair balance, he may recommend that no modification would be

---

66 NPACA 1949, Sch 1A, para 2(2). Coastal Access Reports (Consideration and Modification Procedure) (England) Regulations 2010 (SI 2010/1976), reg 3 and Sch 1 have specified: British Association for Shooting and Conservation, British Mountaineering Council, Country Land and Business Association, National Farmers Union, Open Spaces Society, Ramblers' Association, Royal Society for the Protection of Birds, Persons with sporting rights over the affected land.

67 NPACA 1949, Sch 1A, paras 7 and 8.

68 NPACA 1949, Sch 1A, para 9.

69 NPACA 1949, Sch 1A, para 12.

70 I.e. those matters specified in NPACA 1949 Sch 1A, para 3(3)(a)–(f).

71 NPACA 1949, Sch 1A, para 10. Coastal Access Reports (Consideration and Modification Procedure) (England) Regulations 2010 (SI 2010/1976), reg 5. See also regs 6, 7, 8 and 9 on the appointed person's functions in relation to objections and representations.

effective to do so, or that a certain modification would or might do so. Where he considers no modification would strike a fair balance, he may make suggestions which would or might mitigate the failure.

The appointed person may make his determination after a public inquiry[72] or hearing or on the basis of written representations.[73]

The Secretary of State, before deciding whether to approve the proposals in a coastal report, may identify or investigate possible modifications to the report.[74]

Before approving proposals in respect of a coastal access report[75] the Secretary of State must consider any admissible objections, Natural England's comments on them, the appointed person's report, any representations and Natural England's comment on them and any information or documents requested from Natural England by the appointed person. The Secretary of State may approve proposals relating to one or more parts of the route only, whilst rejecting other proposals.

The Secretary of State will be bound by the finding of facts in the report of the appointed person, except where: (1) the finding involves an assessment of the significance of a matter to any person with a relevant interest in the land or to the public; (2) there was insufficient evidence to make the finding; (3) the finding was made by reference to irrelevant factors or without regard to relevant ones; or (4) the finding was otherwise perverse or irrational.[76]

The Secretary of State must take reasonable steps to give notice of the determination of the coastal access report to those with a relevant interest in the affected land or where he considers it appropriate to publish such notification. He must also notify his determination to Natural England, and to every National Park authority, joint planning board, county council, county borough council and district council whose park or area is traversed by the route to which the report relates, any London borough council for an area in which affected land is situated, any relevant local access forum, the Historic Buildings and Monuments Commission for

---

72 NPACA 1949, Sch 1A, para 13: the inquiry or hearing will be governed by the Local Government Act 1972.

73 Coastal Access Reports (Consideration and Modification Procedure) (England) Regulations 2010 (SI 2010/1976), Pt 5 sets out the procedure where an objection is considered at a public inquiry or hearing.

74 NPACA 1949, Sch 1A, para 15. Coastal Access Reports (Consideration and Modification Procedure) (England) Regulations 2010 (SI 2010/1976), Pt 4 covers the procedure where the Secretary of State has proposals for modification.

75 Under NPACA 1949, s 52.

76 NPACA 1949, Sch 1A, para 16.

England and the Environment Agency. Where there were objections, the Secretary of State must give reasons for his determination so far as it is relevant to the objection. He must also give reasons if he does not follow a recommendation in the report.[77]

Wide powers are given to the Secretary of State to make regulations on most aspects of the procedures.[78]

Where Natural England proposes a variation to approved proposals, the procedural requirements apply with necessary modifications.[79] If the Secretary of State considers that a variation should be made but no proposal has been made by Natural England, he may, by regulations, provide the modifications which are to apply to the procedural requirements. He may not make a direction for a variation if there are no regulations in force.

10.8 Access preparation period

There will be a period of time between the approval of a coastal route and the right of access coming into force, being a day appointed by the Secretary of State by order in relation to the particular stretch of coast covered by the report.[80] This is to enable Natural England to do any necessary work to make the route or routes suitable for public access. There may be gates or steps to install, signs or notices to erect and directions to make for exclusions or restrictions which will come into force at the end of the preparation period.

Land which already qualifies as access land, being mapped open country or registered common land, will continue to be treated as such until the end of the preparation period. This means that existing rights of access and any exclusions or restrictions will apply to the land during that time. The position on occupiers' liability will remain unchanged so that the more limited liability for land which is coastal margin will not apply until the end of the preparation period.

At the end of the preparation period, any existing exclusions or restrictions will cease to have effect,[81] and the regime governing land which is coastal margin will come into effect. There may be a direction for new exclusions or restrictions.

---

77 NPACA 1949, Sch 1A, para 17.

78 See NPACA 1949, Sch 1A, paras 2, 3(7), 10(6) 14, 15 and 16.

79 NPACA 1949, s 55H, but s 55(3) does not apply.

80 MCAA 2009, s 303(6).

81 MCAA 2009, s 303(7).

If the land has been dedicated as coastal margin before the order came into force, the land is treated as coastal margin by virtue of the dedication. This means that the access preparation period does not apply.

10.9 Temporary diversions

Natural England may establish a temporary route if the English coastal route or an official alternative route is closed by an exclusion.[82] It may not do so if the direction is for a permanent exclusion. In such a case, Natural England would propose a variation of the route.[83]

Natural England may give a direction specifying a route and its duration. The temporary route may pass only over: (1) access land; (2) land accessible to the public under section 15 of the CROWA 2000; (3) a highway; and (4) any other land where the owner has given his consent and the Environment Agency has been consulted.

The direction must be in writing and may be revoked or varied by a subsequent direction.

10.10 The right of access to coastal margin

The right of the public to enter and remain on access land, which is coastal margin, is similar to the right of access to mapped open country and registered common land. The main differences in relation to land which is coastal margin, as distinct from other access land, are as follows:

(1) If there is a prohibition against access in any enactment, there will be no right of access. In the case of other access land, a prohibition in a local or private Act will not prevent access.[84]

(2) The general restrictions in Schedule 2 to the CROWA 2000 are modified. Fishing-related conduct on land which is coastal margin is permitted. 'Fishing-related conduct' means having a fishing rod or line or engaging in activities which are connected with, or ancillary to, fishing with a rod or line, or with a line only in exercise of the right to fish provided the activities do not take place on land used for grazing or other agricultural purposes.[85]

---

82 NPACA 1949, s 55I.

83 Under NPACA 1949, s 55.

84 CROWA 2000, s 2(3) and (3A).

85 Access to the Countryside (Coastal Margin) (England) Order 2010 (SI 2010/558), Sch 1, Pt 2, para 12.

(3) There are additional rules on dogs. Dogs are not allowed on coastal margin unless the dog is under effective control. 'Effective control' means that the dog is on a lead or within sight and the person in control has reason to be confident that the dog will return promptly and reliably on command. The dog must remain on access land or on other land to which that person has a right of access. A dog in tidal waters is regarded as remaining on access land.[86]

(4) An extra restriction applies to coastal margin land only. A person is not entitled to be on such land, if, on that land, he obstructs any person passing, or attempting to pass, on foot along any part of the English coastal route, or any official alternative or temporary route.[87]

10.11 Liabilities

10.11.1 Natural England and the Secretary of State

No duty of care in negligence is owed to any person by Natural England, or anyone acting on its behalf, such as employees or agents, when preparing, proposing or varying the coastal route,[88] or in any failure by it to erect signs and notices warning of obstacles or hazards.[89] It is expected that Natural England will place warning signs only where it is aware of an obstacle or hazard which is unusual or cannot easily be identified by the public.[90]

Nor is there any duty of care where Natural England fails to impose an exclusion or restriction under Chapter II of Part I of the CROWA 2000. However, the duty of care is not removed when Natural England decides not to act where there is an application for a direction for the purposes of land management,[91] protection against fire or avoiding danger to the public.[92] There could also be liability where Natural England does not act in accordance with representations made after

86 Access to the Countryside (Coastal Margin) (England) Order 2010 (SI 2010/558), Sch 1, Pt 2, paras 13 and 14.

87 Access to the Countryside (Coastal Margin) (England) Order 2010 (SI 2010/558), Sch 1, Pt 2, para 14.

88 Under NPACA 1949, s 51 or s 55.

89 Under MCAA 2009, Sch 20, para 6(2)(b).

90 MCAA 2009, s 305(1).

91 Under CROWA 2000, s 24.

92 Under CROWA 2000, s 25.

consultation with the original applicant before revoking or varying such directions.[93]

The Secretary of State owes no duty of care in negligence when approving, or giving a direction for the variation of, proposals for a coastal long-distance route.[94]

10.11.2 Occupiers' liability

A person who enters land in exercise of rights granted by the CROWA 2000 does not count as a visitor for the purposes of the Occupiers' Liability Act. The occupier does owe a duty of care, similar to that owed to trespassers under the Occupiers' Liability Act 1984. However, any duty, in respect of a risk resulting from a natural feature of the landscape, or of any river, stream, ditch or pond, whether or not a natural feature, is excluded. Where land is coastal margin, including land dedicated as such, the exclusion of liability is extended to any physical feature. This would include any man-made feature, such as wartime defences.[95] The exclusion of liability does not apply to anything done intentionally or recklessly by the landowner.

If a person enters land as a trespasser and not in exercise of his right of access under section 2(1) of the CROWA 2000 (e.g. because there is an exclusion or restriction forbidding access), the duty of care under the Occupiers' Liability Act 1984 will not be reduced but will extend to natural and man-made features in the normal way.

There is also the possibility of liability for owners and occupiers of land and keepers of livestock under other legislation such as the Animals Act 1971 and the Health and Safety legislation.

10.12 Wales

The coastal access provisions in Part 9 of the MCAA 2009 apply to England only. However, the Act[96] amends the Government of Wales Act 2006 to enable the National Assembly for Wales to establish and maintain a route or a number of routes for the coast to allow the public to make recreational journeys. It does not include a power to create

93 MCAA 2009, s 305(2).

94 MCAA 2009, s 305(4).

95 MCAA 2009, s 306.

96 MCAA 2009, s 310.

new highways by Assembly Measure, nor to allow access by mechanically propelled vehicles other than invalid carriages.

The National Assembly may also secure access to relevant land for the purposes of open-air recreation. Land is relevant if it is at the coast or can be used in association with that land or with the coastal routes.

'Coast' means the coast of Wales adjacent to the sea, including the coast of any island. The sea includes the upstream waters of a river, being the waters from the seaward limit of the estuarial waters of the river to the first public foot crossing, whether by bridge or tunnel.

11 Further Reading

11.1 Books

John Riddall and John Trevelyan, *Rights of Way: A Guide to Law and Practice* (4th edn, Ramblers' Association and Open Spaces Society, 2007)

Stephen Sauvain, *Highway Law* (5th edn, Sweet and Maxwell, 2013)

Angela Sydenham, *Public Rights of Way and Access to Land* (4th edn, Jordan Publishing Ltd, 2010)

Halsbury's Laws of England (4th edn, LexisNexis), Volume 21, Highways, Streets and Bridges

11.2 Government guidance

Appeal a right of way decision:

www.gov.uk/appeal-right-of-way-decision

Definitive map orders, consistency guidelines:

www.gov.uk/government/publications/definitive-map-orders-consistency-guidelines

Planning Inspectorate Advice Notes:

www.gov.uk/government/collections/rights-of-way-advice-notes

Rights of Way Circular 1/09, 'Guidance for Local Authorities':

www.gov.uk/government/publications/rights-of-way-circular-1-09

Rights of Way Guidance Booklet: Guidance on procedures for considering objections to definitive map and public path orders:

www.gov.uk/government/publications/rights-of-way-guidance-booklet

Index

References are to page numbers.